THE
LEAN
ENTERPRISE

THE
LEAN
ENTERPRISE

Designing and Managing
Strategic Processes
for Customer-Winning
Performance

Dan Dimancescu
Peter Hines
Nick Rich

AMACOM
American Management Association

New York • Atlanta • Boston • Chicago • Kansas City • San Francisco • Washington, D.C.
Brussels • Mexico City • Tokyo • Toronto

Library of Congress Cataloging-in-Publication Data

Dimancescu, Dan.
    The lean enterprise : designing and managing strategic processes
  for customer-winning performance / Dan Dimancescu, Peter Hines, Nick
  Rich.
        p.   cm.
    Includes index.
    ISBN 0-8144-0365-4 (hard)
      1. Industrial management.   2. Business planning.
  3. Organizational change.   4. Communication in management.
  5. Industrial management—Case studies.   I. Hines, Peter.
  II. Rich, Nick.   III. Title.
  HD31.D534   1997
  658.4′012—dc21   97-3891
                                                CIP

Printing number

10   9   8   7   6   5   4   3   2   1

To
Katherine, Jane, and **Fiona**
for their patience and support

CONTENTS

CONTENTS

CONTENTS

FOREWORD

Managers are exhausted by programs and tired of techniques! Yet they know that "the times they are a-changing"—and the sand is shifting under their feet. What worked yesterday no longer works today. Customers are more demanding, competitors are sharper on their feet, and new markets and new competitors are emerging in East Asia to challenge them.

Most of the new management recipes over the last ten years have run their course without having a lasting impact on the bottom line. They come—and they go. Employees just await for managers to lose interest and move to the next initiative. Middle managers juggle change programs and steal resources to implement those whose champions shout the loudest. Top management uses change programs to bargain for resources in the annual corporate planning round, but rarely does it stop to disentangle the results of its programs from the many other shocks that rock the business during the year.

The authors of this book show that change is itself critical to corporate survival and needs to be explicitly managed as a central process of the business. They present a very powerful three-tiered system for deciding on the direction the business needs to take, focusing resources only on activities that will generate the biggest gains and translating objectives into shop-floor projects with clear performance improvement targets. This three-tier approach works! In my view, it is one of the most powerful tools to make real change happen.

But no organization is an island. Each company contributes but a piece of the final value purchased by the customer, so it is vital that this three-tier change process be extended to include the most important allies in the shared value creation process. Easier said than done! This book not only describes what needs to be done but also shows how many companies have successfully established supplier associations to align and remove waste from their joint value streams.

This book helps close the gap between the rhetoric—which well-known company does not claim to have embraced the magic recipes?—and the reality: marginal throughput time, inventories, total cost, market share, and profits. The examples used in the pages ahead provide a clear map for managers looking for a way to really enhance the future for their company and their customers.

Professor *Daniel T. Jones*
Coauthor, *The Machine That Changed the World* and *Lean Thinking,* and Director of the Lean Enterprise Research Centre at Cardiff Business School, University of Wales

ACKNOWLEDGMENTS

Our gratitude is shared with the many individuals, companies, research institutions, and consultants that helped in the development of this book.

Special thanks to colleagues at the Technology and Strategy Group in Cambridge, Massachusetts; the Institute for Man and Technology in Nantes, France; the School of Management at Boston University; and the Lean Enterprise Research Centre at Cardiff Business School, University of Wales. The latter include Dan Jones, whose words appear in the Foreword, Rebecca Eley, Sara Bragg, and Roger Mansfield. The roll call of thanks includes Yves Thomas of Atlantech, Kemp Dwenger of InterMatrix and the International Association for Product Development, Mike McMaster of Knowledge Based Development, James Womack and Don Clausing of the Massachusetts Institute of Technology, David Burt of San Diego State University, Masayoshi Okeda of Chuo University, Toshio Niwa and Atsushi Ideta of the Institute for International Economic Studies, and Thierry Consigny of the EC-Japan Center. Also to be thanked are Paul Morris of Supplier Association Partners, John Moon of Stratagem, Tony Thomas, and program managers of the Welsh Development Agency.

Special thanks to the many companies with whom the authors have maintained a relationship and whose experiences are described in the pages that follow, including the Trane Company, a Division of American Standard, Hewlett-Packard, Mitel, and Pilkington Optronics. We are grateful to the companies that participated in the Supply Chain Development Program, including Bass Brewers, Birds

Eye Walls (Unilever), Britvic Soft Drinks, Calsonic Radiators, Clarks International, Dalgety Food Ingredients, IBM, ICI Chemicals and Polymers, Kuwait Petroleum, Lever Brothers, London Underground, Nortel, Pedigree Petfoods, RS Components, Tesco Stores, Unipart, Cander Burgh Foods, and the Welsh Health Common Services Authority. Within these organizations, special thanks are due to Lyndon Jones, Archie Dempster, Andy Dixon, Kevin, Hall, Elaine Haddock, Keith Pacey, David Noble, Ian Kellie, and Graham Booth for their generous time and interest. Corporate insights were also gleaned from the valuable assistance of Borg Warner Automotive, in particular its Margam, South Wales, facility, management and teams; Rover Group Limited; TRW Steering Systems Limited; The Lane Group; GM Windsor Trim facility; Nissan UK, David Jones and Jim Taylor at Trico; and the many staff at Toyota in various plants around the world.

For details about this book or its authors, please contact: Dan Dimancescu, TSG, Harvard Square, PO Box 381347, Cambridge, Massachusetts (Telephone: 617-497-1111; e-mail: tsgdd@aol.com).

INTRODUCTION

Most executives are confronted with the need to change day in and day out. Sales might be flat, a competitor has suddenly made off with a key client, defense cutbacks hit, a new technology that was on the horizon has just appeared as a product that makes yours obsolete, shareholders are clamoring for growth, a new regulation goes into effect. There will always be answers to such dilemmas—but not necessarily in time to help the company in need of them. Our contribution through this book is to serve as observers, catalysts, and innovators. By seeing and interpreting what works in other companies, we can help change-minded managers apply successful techniques within their own organizations.

Hence the theme of this book: how to tame the growing complexity of day-to-day business and thus profitably deliver goods and services valued by customers. The subject is not new. What *is* new is a "strategic process" framework that entered the Western corporate mainstream in the 1990s. It is an antidote to a fragmented and departmentalized system of management that no longer delivers effective solutions in a fast-moving global economy. A rapidly evolving view of management turns the old on end by treating organizations as whole entities first and considering the parts second. Put another way, managers are learning to think and act systemically. Process management is one important manifestation of that learning.

Examples of process-driven companies, with which we have had firsthand experience, span the United States, Japan, and parts of Europe. Many of the fundamentals of process management were pioneered in Japan in the 1960s, but the concepts did not gain serious corporate attention in the United States until the late 1980s, fueled by a wave of interest in process reengineering. The same interest took hold in Europe starting a few years later. But what we describe herein has less to do with process reengineering than it does with an entirely new perception of competition based on leveraging organization-wide knowledge and on a capacity to innovate. Both call for information-intensive activities that put a very different premium on the roles, competencies, and interrelationships of employees.

At the same time, a more subtle but growing corporate interest in the applicability of complexity theory has helped illuminate some of the critical features of emerging management systems. Of these, the most central is an awareness of nonlinear relationships, which are neither sequential nor narrowly task-based, as a defining feature of the new enterprise. What it means is that as businesses find themselves engaging in more complex activities, it becomes more and more difficult to control any one individual or actor in the process. This makes clearly definable outcomes less and less predictable because activities are no longer linear or sequentially predictable sums. This realization is at the core of process management as we define it. The reader is thus alerted to the bias of this book toward nonlinearity of interrelationships as a critical ingredient to the functioning of a lean enterprise.

In the detail, however, the reader may be surprised to find a number of examples drawn from companies in Wales, a sparsely settled region with three million inhabitants concentrated in two industrial bands, one to the west of Manchester, England, and another in the south around Cardiff, the capital. Although the emphasis is because two authors are residents of Wales, more important, Wales has become an exceptional case of rapid economic development in Europe—a "minimotor," as observers are prone to coin such areas. This is attributed to a dynamic governmental development agency, a skilled but cheap labor pool, and a growing agglomeration of transplanted companies from at least a dozen countries. As many as forty-five of these have Japanese parentage. These circumstances have seeded a unique and innovative hotbed in which new management ideas are being absorbed and yet newer ones are being generated in hybrid form. Hence our inclusion of Welsh companies as case studies of organizations in the process of moving from a dying nineteenth- and twentieth-century industrial infrastructure to one adapted to global competitive standards.

We have divided the book into several parts. These can be read as "chunks" of content, or, alternatively, as single chapters that appear pertinent. In that case, we recommend perusal of the first chapter, because it sets the context or framework for all the chapters that follow. Chapters contained in Part I explore the character and practice of process management with a strong emphasis on nonlinearity of working relationships as a defining feature. Its centerpiece is the three-tier teaming system. Visible in companies as large as Hewlett-Packard, Milliken, and Analog Devices, the system thrives with diminished departmental or functional hierarchies and with a keen application of metrics, or benchmarks, as a means of maintaining focus and pacing the rate of change. Part II offers insight through the doers at each of the three tiers: senior management, process owners, and action teams. An underlying theme is the delegation of authority and decision making throughout the organization. Part III takes a panoramic view of two core customer-facing processes: order fulfillment and new product development. Strong emphasis is also given to the growing practice of treating suppliers as partners sharing commercial risks and opportunities. Of particular interest is the phenomenon of "supplier associations" and a unique experiment building such groups in Wales and England. In Part IV, cases describe the journey two companies embarked on in moving to process-driven competitive strategies. Part V opens the door to a next step in the evolution of the modern corporation. Finally, Appendix B contains prescriptive how-to methodologies that will be of practical interest to readers.

This work is preceded by the coauthors' substantial investigative and applied work. Both Dimancescu and Hines spent considerable time in Japan on exploratory visits. Dimancescu's *The Seamless Enterprise: Making Cross-Function Management Work* (1992) and Hines's *Creating World Class Suppliers* (1994) were influenced by the authors' findings and by Western adaptations of them that the authors helped introduce. Those activities influenced both individuals to engage in shared-learning consortia, albeit in different but complementary guises. In 1990 Dimancescu helped found, and codirected, the International Association for Product Development (IAPD), a consortium of Fortune 500 electronics companies. Its goal was to probe the world of horizontal process management and identify best practices in product development in Japan, the United States, and Europe. Five years of findings were summarized in *World Class New Product Development: Benchmarking Best Practices of Agile Manufacturers* (1996). Hines, in a parallel course, pioneered the creation of supplier associations in Wales, an effort in which he collaborated with Rich, a colleague at the Lean Enterprise Research Centre at the University of Wales's Cardiff Business School. Both have the added benefit of having worked in numerous cases at the shop-floor level, close to individuals and teams whose labor and judgment, in the final analysis, make or break the best-conceived strategies and plans.

In parallel with the IAPD network, Hines and Rich, supported by university colleagues at Cardiff and Bath, brought together twenty of Europe's leading exponents of "lean thinking" through the Supply Chain Development Program (SCDP). These innovators are drawn from retailing, automotive, electronics, clothing, process, and service industries. All share a common interest: They want to be the best in what they are doing. Many examples and anecdotes about process-focused change are drawn from these companies.

The substantive ideas underlying the concepts of process-driven management have been explored over the years through an evolutionary chain of lean-thinker meetings initiated by Dimancescu. The first three of these were held at the Thayer School of Engineering at Dartmouth College between 1988 and 1993. They were followed by two similar meetings at the Abbaye de Villeneuve in 1994 and 1996 with the support of the Institute for Man and Technology in Nantes, France. To those were invited a mix of executives (business and military), intellectuals from the social and hard sciences, philosophers, and systems theorists. The intent was to create an informal setting for a dialogue on evolving organizational concepts.

Throughout all these activities—and indeed at the heart of this book—is the intent of being pragmatic while remaining at the cutting edge of new ideas. The result is not a book of management theory but rather a description of an emerging style of management in which process-driven excellence is the strategy.

The model of management we have right now is the opera. The conductor of an opera has a very large number of different groups that he has to pull together. The soloists, the chorus, the ballet, the orchestra, all have to come together—but they have a common score. What we are increasingly talking about today are diversified groups that have to write the score while they perform.

What you need now is a jazz group. And when you have a really good jazz group, how large can it be?

Peter Drucker, *Wired Magazine,* August 1996

PART I

Seeing
the
Whole

Chapter 1

THE VITAL FEW

Organizations are not built to serve customers; they are built to preserve internal order. To customers, the internal structure may not only mean very little, it may serve as a barrier. Organization charts are vertical, and serving the customer is horizontal.

George Fisher, former CEO of Motorola (now CEO of Kodak)

Sometime in the early 1990s, the word *process* became part of mainstream executive language. With the new buzzword came a new landscape of lean managerial capabilities, concepts, behavior, and language. Winning in business would never be quite the same again. Holistic methods and tools would surface as a result of new understandings of teams as composites of skills necessary to deal with increasingly complex problems.

For many companies, aligning organizational competencies around a vital few core processes has become a competitive strategy. By doing so, the most visionary business leaders are recognizing that it is processes, not functions or departments, that deliver customer value and satisfaction. These processes have two purposes: One is to "qualify" your company in the eyes of a buyer; the other is to demonstrate a capability that will "win an order."[1] Do either of these poorly or less well than the competitor next door, and you are out of business. Processes that meet basic quality, cost, and delivery expectations, for example, are all order qualifiers with outcomes that can be precisely measured. Each establishes a reason why a buyer will, or will not, consider buying from you. For example, a customer might define a measure such as 50 ppm (parts per million) to govern the management of the quality process, or use a time-based measure for the delivery of a product. Such measures define the competitive battleground. If a company does not qualify because it cannot meet those requirements, it is unlikely to generate business with the customer.

Winning an order, the second purpose, is an outcome of processes that significantly exceed customer expectations and excite the customer. Order winners can include vastly superior levels of quality, cost, or delivery as well as features or services that differentiate the product and benefit the customer. Such differentiators are often a result of mastery over a critical innovative capability such as an ability to customize products, a fast time-to-market, the establishment of an electronic data interchange (EDI) link with the customer so that the two companies can communicate seamlessly, or new methods of streamlining and removing time or materials waste in a transaction.

Although the single processes that cut across organizational boundaries may be labeled with a variety of names, they fall into a few generic categories. Denis Welch, general manager of Pilkington Optronics's Saint Asaph's operations in Wales, conceptualized his core processes by drafting a simple sketch (Figure 1.1) and presenting it at a work session where his executive team was wrestling with a worldwide downturn in defense contracts. On one side, the sketch showed the traditional organizational pyramid, in which skills and competencies at Pilkington were owned by functions. On the other, it showed three customer-facing lateral processes, each of which focused the competencies of the company on meeting a business outcome: getting new orders, responding to needs, introducing new products. These three key processes defined, in his view, the company's strategic capabilities. Welch's aim was to achieve superior competitive performance, not by managing *who* was on the functional organization chart but by managing *how* value was delivered to the company's customers.

1.1. Task-focused vs. process-focused strategies.

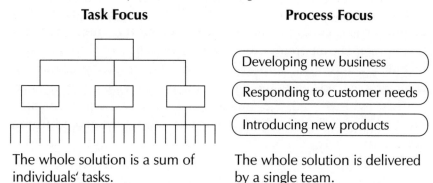

Task Focus	Process Focus

The whole solution is a sum of individuals' tasks.

The whole solution is delivered by a single team.

Welch's sketch would later generate a lively debate within the parent company's executive team. The question was whether it should institute a companywide "order capture" process spanning its small-business unit. Such discussions underscore the fact that teaming around key processes starts at the top with the CEO and the executive team. Their first responsibility is to map a strategy and then manage the portfolio of core processes necessary to achieve their goals. However, for most managers the execution of a process-focused strategy requires a wholly new commitment and collaborative skills, which are not always present. A study cited in *Planning Review* (November 1990) of 500 American executives in technology-based companies revealed that 80 percent of them did not understand how key processes work. How then could they be expected to manage them without substantial training?

THE BIG FOUR: Q, C, D, AND PRODUCT DEVELOPMENT

Those who understood the potential of a process-focused strategy realized it could unleash new levels of productivity unmatched by functionally structured organizations. The pioneers got an early foothold in Japan at companies such as Toyota and Komatsu, which experimented in cross-organizational teaming early in the 1960s. Four primary processes, vital to an organization's survival, were identified, each with outcomes of critical importance to the customer. They were labeled Quality, Cost, Delivery, and New Product Development—known for short as QCD management. Another category of processes was identified as "secondary," meaning that it was of internal importance to the competitiveness of the business. It included such things as information management, personnel training, and research and development. All of these strategic processes are journeys without end. Regardless of the operating environment of the company, it is unlikely that any one can be dissociated from a competitive strategy. They are the bedrock on which the success of the lean global corporation is founded.

The *quality* process focuses on meeting customer requirements and on minimizing warranty costs. It addresses the question, Does the product meet the expected customer requirements? Because doing so calls for interactions crossing many traditional functional boundaries and invariably includes suppliers, the process is managed by a team representing all the relevant functions.

The *cost* process seeks to strip out excess cost wherever it might exist in the organization. Rather than issuing a one-size-fits-all top-down directive that all departments reduce their costs by a particular percentage, the process team designs a system that will optimize the continuous reduction of cost within all parts of the organization and its allied suppliers. This allows the company to achieve increasingly stringent levels of price competitiveness by treating the effort system-ically.

Delivery process teams (more commonly referred to as order fulfillment in the West) manage the time and quantity elements involved in sourcing materials, producing, and getting the product or service delivered as desired by a customer. As companies have moved closer and closer to Just-In-Time (JIT), Efficient Consumer Response (ECR), Quick Response Logistics (QRL), and rapid new product Time To Market (TTM), this cross-functional process has become vitally important in generating competitive advantage from time-based competitive strategies. Electronic links now make "real time" delivery a reality. One can, for example, use the Internet to order software, pay for it, and download it ready for use, all within minutes.

New product development (also referred to as the innovation process) is a cross functional process that seeks to maximize a company's success rate in new product introduction. Japanese automotive assemblers, such as Toyota, Nissan, and Honda, made substantial breakthroughs by involving suppliers in partnering design and investment risks within targeted costs and performance specifications. Calsonic Llanelli Radiators, a Welsh first-tier supplier to Nissan-Europe, for example, invested heavily in state-of-the-art product design capabilities for its "under the hood" new product introductions as a competitive differentiator.

Process teams helped promote optimization of the whole company's performance by aligning interests across the company. The integration of both vertical responsibilities (functional departments) and horizontal responsibilities (cross-functional management) became colloquially known as the warp and woof system (alluding to textile weaving, where strength is created by tightly weaving threads in two directions). This approach created a mutually reinforcing management method focused on tackling competitive priorities derived from the strategic business plan. Dr. Kenji Kurogane, recipient of the Deming Prize and counselor to the Japanese Standards Association and to the Japanese Union of Scientists and Engineers (JUSE), characterized this as a bold step away from delegating responsibility narrowly within departments: "In a companywide system . . . managers were assigned to multiple cross-functional areas in such a way as to promote the analysis of activities from a companywide point of view."[2]

It was only in 1988, that JUSE decided a definition was needed for the cross-functional system many companies had embraced. They described it as

> a management process designed to encourage and support interdepartmental communication and co-operation throughout a company—as opposed to command and control through narrow departments or divisions. The purpose is to attain such company-wide targets as quality, cost, and delivery of products and services by optimizing the sharing of work.

For the strategist, these core processes represent order qualifiers and order winners. This is what companies such as Toyota and Komatsu realized early in the 1960s as they struggled to overcome inferior product images and less than capable manufacturing. Only through effective coordination between the parent company's departments and a large infrastructure of suppliers would there be any hope of reaching standards necessary to capture significant markets in the United States. This coordination was achieved through a cross-organizational structure of process teams focused predominantly on quality, cost, delivery, and new product development. QCD management became the familiar label for a management style eventually propagated widely within large Japanese manufacturing companies during the 1970s and 1980s. Coupled with the fundamentals of total quality embraced from U.S. business gurus and embellished upon with Japanese discipline, a potent new form of lean management ensued. It allowed vital export-focused sectors such as machine tools, automobiles, and consumer electronics to belt-tighten to unusual extremes when pushed to the wall by the oil shock of the 1970s and later by the rapid devaluation of the dollar against the yen.

❖ Only through effective coordination between the parent company's departments and a large infrastructure of suppliers would there be any hope of reaching standards necessary to capture significant markets in the United States.

A study of Deming Prize winners completed in the late 1980s ranked Japanese use of strategic processes as shown in Figure 1.2. Each is managed by cross-organizational teams. Of interest is the very low priority given to information control, an area in which Japanese companies have been slower to make world-class inroads than American or European companies. Supplier partnerships are embedded in many of these cross-organizational processes.

The *supplier partnership* embedded in these core processes creates mutual benefit through shared responsibility and risk. The growth of

1.2. Japanese use of strategic processes.

Core Process	Functions Encompassed	Number of Companies
Quality	Quality control, Warranty improvement	59
Cost control	Profit control Expense control Cost cuts	54
Delivery control	Product quantity control, Delivery data control, Production system, Factory control, Manufacturing data control	39
Product development	Research and development Technical development Production techniques	22
Sales control	Marketing, Sales activities control, Order control, Sales promotion	14
Personnel control	Talent development, Education	11
Safety control	Safety and sanitary control, Labor safety environmental control	7
Purchase control	Order control	6
Other	QC promotion control	3
	Information control	3
	Future planning	2

strategic partnerships was accelerated by a growing awareness that traditional purchasing practices of holding multiple vendor bases caused serious inefficiency and lowered supply chain performance. A secondary rationale for supplier partnerships is that, without such a relationship, no customer can ever know enough about a supplier, and vice versa, to take full advantage of both parties' combined resources and expertise. The migration of such partnerships to North America and Europe is described in more detail in Chapter 12.

❖ No customer can ever know enough about a supplier, and vice versa, to take full advantage of both companies' combined resources and expertise.

An example of Japanese-style strategic process management can be seen at the British automobile assembly facility of Nissan Corporation. It was one of the first Japanese corporations to locate outside of Japan, calling for an investment of more than $1.4 billion at the Sunderland, England, site. Manufacturing 240,000 vehicles a year, the plant is regarded as a jewel in the Nissan global empire. Producing models under the local names Micra and Primera, Nissan launched a new program under the code EQ, the project name given to the vehicle intended to replace the Primera. This vehicle represented a groundbreaking initiative by the company because most of the car's design and parts would come from current suppliers in the United Kingdom and on the European continent.

On first arriving in the United Kingdom, Nissan was faced with European Union restrictions regarding the content of the vehicles assembled. The amount of European-supplied product had to equal 80 percent of the value of the final product. Thus, Nissan confronted not only the risk associated with the development of a new assembly facility and the recruitment of a workforce without traditional automotive skills but also the requirement of sourcing products from a supply base that had not been exposed to JIT principles or the stringent requirements of Japanese vehicle production.

To support the production of vehicles, the company carefully assessed the sources of local supply, initially looking for companies that could demonstrate a will to perform and a cultural "fit" with Nissan. The result of this search created an initial base of 198 suppliers. The number alone was dramatically smaller than traditional European supply bases to a single company, which can number in the thousands—or five to ten times more. Having selected the suppliers according to order-qualifying criteria, however, the company was faced with aligning the assorted suppliers with the business plan of the facility and the performance measures imposed from Japanese headquarters.

In 1993, the company launched a supplier development program termed NX96, or simply World Class in 1996. The goal was "to support Nissan UK's objectives through the achievement of world-class manufacturing status by [the company's] suppliers—to be measured by supplier performance in OCDD&P [Quality, Cost, Delivery, Design Development, and Supplier Partnership]." The program called on suppliers to adopt, in one leap, a cross-functional process structure as a competitive driver, thereby mirroring Nissan's own. The supplier side was to be championed by the purchasing department, which in turn was responsible to the supplier subgroup within the company. In the company's words, "the purchasing department, through the management group, coordinates cross-functional activities to establish and monitor detailed business plan reviews, joint objectives, and improvement plans." Improvement requirements could thus be cascaded down into the overall supply base management scores, joint improvement plans, annual business plan reviews, joint objective setting, and a documented strategy to support NX96.

Thus, Quality, Cost, Delivery, Design Development, and Supplier Partnership provided the common process frame of reference for all suppliers, regardless of size, technology employed, or geographical location. Business ability was defined by performance in each of these areas. For each process, a series of metrics was developed to show the rate of change, explained in Chapter 5, required by the customer in terms of total customer service and generation of new working practices to enhance the company's performance over the long term.

❖ For each process a series of metrics was developed to show the rate of change required by the customer in terms of total customer service and generation of new working practices to enhance the company's performance over the long term.

An example of Nissan metrics deployed to suppliers is shown in Figure 1.3. Similar performance measures covering all five QCDD&

1.3. NX96 quality objectives.

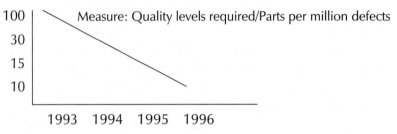

P processes were also given to suppliers in the same manner and with the same level of detail. Each states the quality measure to be applied and the timing for achieving the required performance level. In this fashion, Nissan determined the industry improvement curve for the supply base and thus established a common frame of reference for working with Nissan. To its suppliers, this soon became known as "the Nissan way." As a group, suppliers were made aware of the competitive challenge, the order-qualifying levels, and the future direction of Nissan's needs.

To ensure that the suppliers actually established an infrastructure to support their own lean management system, the company issued information for managers demonstrating how such a system could be implemented. This included the development of strategic business plans by the managing director of the supplying company. The plans contained detailed target measures for all areas of the enterprise; a fully integrated series of processes and their relationship to the business plan, including the levels in the organization covered by the process; and, finally, the methods by which senior managers could ensure complete understanding within the factory.

As the campaign neared the end of this first phase, the foundation for a customer-focused, high-performing system was created. Nissan was quick, too, in acknowledging many of the suppliers' achievements with company awards. Not too long after, Nissan proudly proclaimed that over 10 percent of the supply base to the company exceeded the performance levels of their Japanese counterparts. In this regard, the Nissan site in Sunderland heralded a radical transformation when surveys indicated suppliers' confidence and a positive attitude to a continuing business relationship, despite having to function within one of the most stringent supplier evaluation systems in the industry.

WESTERNIZING STRATEGIC PROCESS MANAGEMENT

Insight into strategic process management reached the United States only late in the 1980s as Japanese "cross-function management"—literally translated as cross-department management—became known through the translation of a breakthrough Japanese text by Dr. Kenji Kurogane.[3] Dan Dimancescu, who translated Kurogane's works privately with funding support from Digital Equipment, wrote the first U.S. book on the same topic, including such U.S. process-minded companies as Boeing and Hewlett-Packard.[4]

Paul Allaire, chairman and CEO of Xerox, is one of the leading proponents of having senior management teams in charge of a process-focused strategy. "You must have a team at the top," he stated. "We always *talked* teams, but today they really are necessary to make companywide processes work effectively. . . . I have six direct reports who form the top management team. But we also have nine division heads, who run their own businesses yet depend on the same laboratories and sales force. They therefore share processes and have to make joint decisions for the betterment of the company. . . . They need to understand [that] their success very much depends on the success of the larger organization and its core processes."[5]

❖ *"We always talked teams, but today they really are necessary to make companywide processes work effectively."*

Wider corporate awareness of strategic process management emerged, too, from a surge in interest in concurrent engineering promoted by the Department of Defense and, later, business process reengineering (BPR), which swept through Western corporations during the first half of the 1990s. First promoted as a means of stripping non–value-added effort out of complex workflow, BPR evolved into a platform advocating cross-organizational process management, much in the form observed in Japanese companies for more than thirty years. In many cases, however, because little training or long-term implementation followed the initial surge of interest, BPR failures started to mount. One of the failings was in the delegation of process "ownership" by the CEO to a single individual, who would then have to battle with functional owners for attention and support. In addition, few companies plunged into process management with the depth of understanding of new managerial behavior required or the recognition that old career tracks would no longer be the measure of individual success.

HOW MILLIKEN & COMPANY GOT STARTED

During the 1980s, the 14,000-person company made substantial strides in quality, which led to its winning the Malcolm Baldrige Quality Award in 1989. Two years later, using an IBM-originated business process management methodology, Milliken & Company took a new look at nineteen core business processes and launched an internally managed benchmarking study that quickly bogged down in a bureaucratic black hole. Looking back on it, one senior executive at Milliken & Company said he felt like he was slowly "descending into hell" with all the bureaucracy. At the same time, a three-week study trip to Japan led to an awareness of a wholly new model of process-focused management and a subsequent decision to go slow on the IBM approach.

Comparing the two approaches, company executives concluded in 1992 that although the IBM processes cut across many organizations, none really had a full enterprisewide impact. In addition, ownership of each of its processes was in the hands of persons directing a single function. Little of the focus of each process had direct bearing on the customer's real stake. A year later, Milliken & Company established its vital few, seven cross-functional process teams (Figure 1.4), the initials of each spelling out QCD IS ME. A senior executive was assigned ownership of each one. The selection reflected what had been observed in Japan but, equally important, characterized "deliverables of the enterprise to its customers." Ken

1.4. Milliken & Company's cross-functional process teams.

Process	Owner
Quality	President of the fashion apparel and specialty fabric division
Cost	President of interior furnishings and LaGrange Industrial Division
Delivery	President of the automotive division
Innovation	President of the fashion fabrics division
Safety	President of spun fabrics division
Morale	General manager of specialty chemicals and packaging
Environment	Director of manufacturing chemicals

Compton, president of Milliken & Company's Automotive Division, was assigned ownership of the corporation delivery process. He stated in an unpublished study team report, "Having each of the senior line managers own a work process has forced us to become dependent on each other and subsequently build alignment on what we must do."

The first three process teams were aimed at continuous improvement in quality, cost, and delivery (QCD). The innovation process (I) stood at the heart of Milliken & Company's vital few because it would be the source of new products as well as improvements for the whole company. The last three teams were seen as providing customer deliverables because consumers are affected by the safety(s) of Milliken & Company's products, by the service that comes from a firm with high morale (M), and by the environmental (E) friendliness of the company's manufacturing processes.

Each team consisted of senior line managers as well as members from such support organizations as quality, education, finance, management information services, and human resources. They shared responsibility for the results of the process and the process measures. One of their first activities was to diagnose how well the process was executed and to evaluate the measurement systems in existence. The latter were found to consistently lead to suboptimal performance and rarely to a customer-focused outcome. In retrospect, these diagnostic efforts were seen as critical to the rapid implementation of QCD IS ME. As one manager put it, "Seeing is believing." Tom Malone, Milliken & Company president, who also led the corporate quality promotion committee, summarized in the study team report the real change he believes has been achieved at Milliken & Company: "Horizontal management is a way to empower senior levels of the company. Before, the team used to wait around until I shared my point of view—which we then typically implemented." He added, "Today, this team meets without me in many cases to formulate their point of view—which now typically 'carries the day.'"

FAMILIES OF PROCESSES

Hewlett-Packard started on the process management path late in the 1980s by building on a precedent of companywide steering councils. These had propagated to almost two dozen—far from being the vital few. Product development became the first candidate, in 1989, for reorganization as a core process. Internal studies had shown it to be fragmented into seventeen different responsibilities. Stu Winby, one of the leaders in conceptualizing new ways of managing, recalled: "We set out to make the product development group the line organization—the functions, all the rest would be staff to them. We wanted to design a team-based work system at a value chain level. This would involve shifting the power base to be horizontal rather than vertical."[6]

Later the company would deepen its skills at process management. Stan Gage, program manager for business process management at Hewlett-Packard's headquarters in Palo Alto, California, pioneered a unique eight-level categorization of processes spanning all activities within a giant global corporation with divisions and business units. Within any one operating unit—whether the corporate parent, a division, a business unit, or a plant—the three-tier system applies.

❖ "We set out to make the product development group the line organization—the functions, all the rest would be staff to them. . . . This would involve shifting the power base to be horizontal rather than vertical."

"Adopting a process review of an organization," said Gage, "represents a revolutionary change in perspective. . . . A hierarchical structure will depict the organizational responsibilities and reporting relationships whereas a process structure depicts a dynamic view of how the organization delivers value."[7] Gage developed a road map of processes that could be found in various levels of a giant global conglomerate such as Hewlett-Packard (Figure 1.5). He ranked these at eight levels, each representing various levels of complexity.

Although Hewlett-Packard may have pioneered the practice of process management in the United States, much as Toyota and Komatsu did in Japan decades earlier, the concepts propagated rapidly to other companies. Emmanuel A. Kampouris, CEO of American Standard, concluded that his corporation needed to redesign the way it went about managing its businesses. Given his aggressive performance expectations of building the price of the company's shares by two-digit multiples, the answer was to reorient around the following five strategic processes. A Westernized version of the QCD model, it included strategy and planning, a category rarely found in Japan:

- Strategy and planning
- Product change and development
- Order obtainment
- Order fulfillment
- Aftermarket customer service

In 1994, these became the basis of a comprehensive reorganization across the company's three operating divisions: Trane (air conditioning), Plumbing Supplies, and Wabco (truck components). Each was required to realign its business around these core processes. A senior executive from each division was delegated to champion a

1.5. Hewlett-Packard process hierarchy.

Level 8	*Companywide* • Processes that affect all elements of an organization (e.g., corporate strategic planning, companywide personnel procedures)
Level 7	*Multiple Businesses Unit* • Processes shared by logical groupings of more than one business unit (e.g., processes used in common by all divisions making computer peripherals)
Level 6	*Single Business Unit* • First level where key cross-departmental processes report (e.g., methods for managing a set of processes that characterize a division)
Level 5	*Portfolio Process* • Methods for managing multiple iterations of any process over time (e.g., product generation process, order fulfillment process)
Level 4	*Single-Process Cycle* • A single iteration of a process from input through output (e.g., product life cycle, shipping a single order)
Level 3	*Activity* • A related group of tasks within a process to produce a result (e.g., circuit design, software test)
Level 2	*Task* • The basic unit of work performed by individuals (e.g., design capture, module functional test, assembly process)
Level 1	*Method* • The basic technique used by individuals to perform work (e.g., analytical technique, automated testing)

process "owned" by a selected senior manager. The executive champion maintained an oversight role while the owner (who was given the title vice-president) took responsibility for designing and monitoring the process. One of the champion's most important roles was to run political interference for the owner when and if called for.

A similar exercise at Xerox showed that four core customer-oriented processes characterized its business:

1. Market to collection
2. Order fulfillment
3. Integrated supply chain
4. Customer service

It was decided that each of these would be managed by teams representing respective functions and competencies, recognizing the inability of any one function or department to act with the needs of the whole system in mind.

CREATING AWARENESS

The first stage in identifying processes needed to create world-class levels of customer satisfaction involves a "health check" of the resources and processes operated by the enterprise and an analysis of how these are combined to offer value to the consumer. In some companies, such as Procter & Gamble, awareness was built by calling on a working task force of middle managers to wipe the slate clean and conceive a wholly new process-focused implementation strategy. In this case, a fourteen-person team, each member maintaining full day-to-day responsibility over his or her line operations, reconceived the company's global supply process. After almost nine months of study, the new process was instituted smoothly and effectively, largely because these same individuals developed a sophisticated leadership training program designed to carry the message of change to their reports, and by their reports to those below them. The success of the whole program rested, at the start, on extensive self-analysis at thirty company sites, benchmarking against almost forty firms, and on studies of about fifty leading consulting and academic frameworks and methodologies.

Such external analyses need to be complemented with a critical assessment of the weaknesses of the current structure and performance of the company. This helps companies avoid being lulled into a false sense of security by stressing only those activities they do well and thus ignoring the inherent weaknesses within the organization.

NOTES

1. The original concept of order winners and order qualifiers can be found in T. Hill, *Manufacturing Strategy: Text and Cases* (Basingstoke, England: Macmillan, 1995).
2. Kenji Kurogane, ed., *Cross-Functional Management: Principles and Practical Applications* (Tokyo: Asian Productivity Organization, 1993).
3. Ibid.
4. *The Seamless Enterprise: Making Cross-Function Management Work* (New York: Wiley, 1994).
5. David A. Garvin, "Leveraging Processes for Strategic Advantage," *Harvard Business Review* (September–October 1995), p. 87.
6. Case study in WDN2 (North Hollywood, Calif.: John Cotter and Associates).
7. Stan Gage, "The Management of Key Enterprise Processes," *Journal of the Center for Quality Management,* spring 1993.

Chapter 2

WHOLE ORGANIZATIONS

We realized our organization had to be redesigned to reflect our strategy, and that's when we began focusing on processes. . . . You can't redesign processes unless you know what you're trying to do. What you are after is congruence among strategic directions, organizational design, staff capabilities, and the processes you use to ensure that people are working together to meet the company's goals.

Paul Allaire, Chairman and CEO of Xerox[1]

There comes a time when complexity of coordination, size of management staff, and operational inflexibility become so overwhelming that hierarchical transmission of all information ceases to be of value.

Paul A. Strassman, *Information Payoff* (New York: Free Press, 1985)

Influencing the change to a process–driven view is the realization that it is the "whole" that must be managed and not just the separate parts. Theorist Ludwig von Bertalanffy pointed this out decades ago. As von Bertalanffy wrote, "In one way or another, we are forced to deal with complexities, with 'wholes' or 'systems', in all fields of knowledge. This implies a basic reorientation in scientific thinking."[2]

More recently, in his best-selling book, Peter Senge of MIT labeled this type of thinking a "fifth discipline" and referred to it as "the cornerstone of how learning organizations think about the world."[3] From such thinking is emerging a cycle of corporate experiments with process-focused management aimed at managing value-adding activity holistically and not as a sum of parts. The basics were first put into practice (as explained in Chapter 1) early in the 1960s in Japan, and the benefits of a cross-organizational system were first reaped in the West starting in the late 1980s by companies like Hewlett-Packard and Unilever. Within a few years holistic management was embraced by other leading companies, such as American Standard, Boeing, Chrysler, Levi Strauss, Milliken, Mitel, Procter & Gamble, Rover Group, Sabre Development Systems (American Airlines), and others.

Behind it all is a systemic approach to dealing with more complex problems as well as with a vastly more demanding customer. At American Standard, for example, the basics of the new approach are introduced in a training program. It leads attendees to ask, What is a system? The answer, with the picture of a car alongside, is "a collection of parts that interact with each other to function as a system." A more complex schematic of a business system is then presented, in which external forces are shown affecting the whole enterprise. Inputs enter the organization, to be filtered through the company's five core processes and create outputs of value to customers. The attendee is asked to ponder ways in which any one variable and feedback loops affect the overall business.

But what does a "systemic" point of view really entail? Ludwig von Bertalanffy offered this explanation: "A certain objective is given; to find ways and means for its realization requires the systems specialist (or team of specialists) to consider alternative solutions and to choose those promising optimization at maximum efficiency and minimal cost in a tremendously complex network of interactions."[4] Or, as later thinkers such as Fritjof Capra would write: "The great shock of twentieth century science has been that systems cannot be understood by analysis. The properties of the parts are not intrinsic properties but can be understood only within the context of the larger hole. . . . Accordingly, systems thinking concentrates not on basic building blocks, but on basic principles of organization."[5] At an accelerating rate, the industrial world has become increasingly aware of the widening scope and value of systemic operating principles. To think and act systemically, the modern manager needs to be keenly aware of four key organizational ingredients (see Figure 2.1) whose interdependencies determine how well a business enterprise will perform in its particular competitive environment (see Figure 2.1). From these ingredients, and the manner in which they are integrated, flow the technological innovations and the products and services that fuel modern economies.

This four-sided organizational model is framed on one side by a linear *task-driven* management style fitting machine-based labor and on the other by a nonlinear *process-driven* style central to a knowledge-intensive economy (see Figure 2.2). In the first instance, the strategy is executed within a rigid top-down prescribed organizational structure (usually depicted as a command and control pyramid). This allows tasks to be determined at the top and then delegated downward according to appropriate roles and responsibilities. In a structure-bound setting, power is expressed by the title an employee holds and where he or she appears in the organization's structure. This power is exercised within tightly demarcated boundaries—"my turf" and "your turf." This approach, a genuine breakthrough when first conceived in the early decades of the twentieth century, caused organizations to waste time and resources in order to produce desired results. Not the least of the toll was a workforce increasingly divorced from any meaningful connectedness to the whole organization. The whole became a collage of parts that lost the ability to respond to aggressive competitive challenges. Workers simply waited to be told what to do.

The new process-based system starts, too, with a well-defined strategy. But it turns next, not to structure, but to identifying vital

2.1. Four key elements of an organizational system.

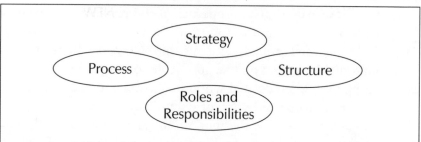

Strategy is a response to external information on competitors, market opportunities, government programs and regulations, and new technologies, as well as an understanding of a firm's internal capabilities and resources. From a well-crafted strategy flows a set of precise objectives revised periodically in reaction to new sources of information.

Processes are patterns of interconnected value-adding relationships designed to meet business goals and objectives. Processes are in a continuous state of change, adapting to both expected and unexpected events. The way in which information is communicated and knowledge is managed affects the quality of decision making and innovation within a process.

Roles and responsibilities are determined in such a way as to carry out key processes. Most valued are individuals who bring specialized competencies and who are able to work with others to solve complex problems. Rewards, career paths, and recognition reinforce the required roles and responsibilities.

Structure reflects the intended strategy and process orientation of an organization. Structure is shaped, too, by geography and by divisional or business unit criteria. However, the dominant feature of the new organizational structure is its emphasis on cross-organizational coordination through process teams and a diminished influence of functions as key components of the structure.

2.2. Task-based vs. process-based management.

THE OLD	THE NEW
Task-based command and control system: strategy *to* structure *to* process tasks *to* roles	Process-based lean system: strategy *to* process *to* roles *to* structure

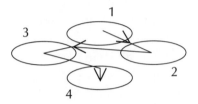 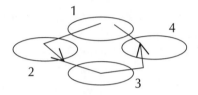

organization-wide processes (or patterns of interconnected relationships between people) that are necessary to deliver value to the customer and thus meet the objectives of the strategy. Appropriate roles, responsibilities, and competencies are then addressed. This requires determining what competencies are most critical and which might be outsourced, and how to stimulate the desired collaborative behavior, leadership, and decision making. "We realized," states Jan Leschly, chief executive of SmithKline Beecham, "that a capability comes only by combining a competence with a reliable process."[6] Only then can a structure be constructed for the processes and competencies that are most appropriate to meeting the strategy and its business objective. Individual parts of an organization are made to feel and act connected to the whole through organization-wide processes. Such connectedness breeds greater motivation, a greater sense of community, and far more proactive commitment to change.

The glue binding these four organizational elements together is the sense of long-term purpose and values communicated to the whole organization by its leaders. This is akin to the seafaring captain declaring his destination in order for his crew to better chart their course. Of course, getting there depends on the quality of teamsmanship that is inspired by the captain and crew. In one exceptional story involving a disastrous fire, effective communication leadership brought all employees in a company to act as a unified team in reacting to the calamity they suddenly and unexpectedly faced.

The fire occurred on a cold night early in December 1995 in Lawrence, Massachusetts, at the Malden Mills, a surprisingly successful survivor of New England's long-gone heyday as the world's leading textile-producing region. In a few hours the mill burned to a blackened shell, and its ability to meet demand for its popular Polartex product vanished in acrid smoke. So did its ability to provide employment and income to its 1,700 workers—just before Christmas. Yet, just two weeks later machines were at work in a neighboring building producing at 70 percent of the mill's earlier capacity. By the end of January it was back to full capacity. The most remarkable figure in this story was the company's owner, Aaron Feuerstein. The day after the fire, he called a meeting of the entire workforce to announce that he would—to their surprise—pay them for the next few weeks—and up to 90 days of necessary—at full wages. And he pledged to bring the mill back to life in Lawrence rather than use the fire as a reason for leaving town and setting up shop in a cheap-labor haven elsewhere.

His compassionate intervention at a critical moment allowed workers, suppliers, bankers, and state officials to mobilize behind a clear vision of a new mill once again alive with activity. Thus when called on in subsequent days and weeks, they were able to adjust and respond *as a whole* to what was a chaotic and unpredictable situation.

❖ They were able to adjust and respond *as a whole* to what was a chaotic and unpredictable situation.

Such abilities do not have to arise solely out of crises. Many companies operate on a basis of continual and radical change. Ask anyone in a Silicon Valley firm as large as Sun Microsystems or Cisco, or as new as Netscape. Their systems of management readjust quickly and effectively to the needs of the marketplace. Change is embraced as a competitive strategy in fast-moving markets; often it is self-inflicted. "One of the signs of a world-class company," said Marc Meyer, a professor at Northeastern University, during a 1995 presentation to the International Association for Product Development, "is its deliberate attempt to obsolete its products and processes before anyone else does." Such organizations exist in a state of continual disequilibrium, always reordering things, a mind–set that runs opposite to a traditional hierarchical managerial instinct bent on maintaining the status quo by "not rocking the boat."

❖ "One of the signs of a world-class company is its deliberate attempt to obsolete its products and processes before anyone else does."

RECURRING PATTERNS OF BEHAVIOR

By observing and comparing successful companies, even those that thrive on continual change, one notes recurring patterns of relationships between people that generate an outcome of some sort. In sports, for example, one talks about defensive or offensive patterns. The pattern will define the degree and quality of interaction between individuals. As James Coplien of AT&T Bell Labs wrote, "A good set of organizational patterns helps (indirectly) to generate the right process."[7] This concept was used by Coplien and colleagues in other companies to effect fundamental changes in the way in which software is developed.

Managers are called on, through this perspective, to take a "patterned" view of their organization, however large or small—to think more like a coach with his x's and o's and a book of patterned plays. The pioneer of patterned thinking, Christopher Alexander, explained the concept of patterns:

> Each pattern describes a problem which occurs over and over again in our environment, and then describes the core of the solution to that problem, in such a way that you can use this solution a million times over, without ever doing it the same way twice.
> Each pattern is connected to certain 'larger patterns which come above it in the language [of patterns]; and to certain 'smaller' patterns which fall below it in the language. . . . In short, no pattern is an isolated entity. Each pattern can exist in the world, only to the extent

that it is supported by other patterns: the larger the pattern in which it is embedded, the patterns of the same size that surround it, and the smaller patterns which are embedded in it.

Each pattern may be looked upon as a hypothesis like one of the hypotheses of science. Each pattern represents our current best guess as to what arrangement . . . will work to solve the problem presented.[8]

Contrasted with a task-based approach, this perspective imparts a very different understanding of how an enterprise works. W. Edwards Deming's famed Plan Do Check Act (PDCA) cycle can be interpreted as a recurring pattern because it calls for certain types of activities to be carried out by a team of people. The PDCA cycle involves no attempt, however, to micromanage the task to be performed. In addition, such things as structure, titles on the door, or functional responsibilities are secondary to the quality of patterns of human interrelationships (or processes) that yield value to a customer. This point highlights two critical success factors: people's competencies and the manner in which information is shared between them. Both call for new management behaviors, new organizational structures, and new support tools for the organization to fully leverage its knowledge-creating potential.

DESIGN PRINCIPLES

Working relationships that appear to yield the greatest performance are rooted in a few fundamental principles. Because these principles affect the interplay of the four key organizational elements introduced earlier—strategy, process, roles and responsibilities, and structure—we refer to them as *design principles*. Once aware of them, the executive can be far more proactive in working to create a highly competitive organization. At least one principle overrides all others as a defining characteristic of the knowledge-intensive, lean enterprise. It is analogous to that of a hologram:

The organization must be designed so that the whole can be seen through any one of the parts—and so that any one part contributes to the whole.

30

Managers can put their organizations to the test by asking this simple question: Can any one employee express the purpose of the whole organization and his or her role in achieving it? This one design principle establishes an organizational frame of reference that influences all else below it. It manifests a systemic view of the organization, the manner in which communication will be carried out, information shared, and value created for customers. "This notion has always been comfortable to me," says Denis Welch, of the Welsh company Pilkington Optronics. "If your expectation is that your people will give you more, they will have to know more about the whole." In his first year as a newly appointed general manager, Welch made a point of meeting with groups of fifty or so employees and sharing in detail the big picture of the company's ambitions, challenges, and expectations. "You'd be amazed how well people react to knowing more about why one might be asking them to work so much harder in meeting stringent cost targets," he observed. "It fills in the blanks and makes the task meaningful."[9]

❖ "If your expectation is that your people will give you more, they will have to know more about the whole."

At Malden Mills (the company in the story about the fire, told earlier in this chapter), its owner helped create an extraordinary organization in which every individual worked with a full appreciation of the whole. Thus, when crisis struck they were able to act and adapt as a cohesive unit. This kind of teamwork is similar to that of a soccer or basketball team at play. At every moment each player on the field or court adjusts positions instantly in reaction to the movement of the ball. As the players move, the actions of the best teams are almost completely reflexive and in constant flux, requiring little input from a coach. The players act as a cohesive unit because each is aware of the whole and can thus act and react accordingly. The coach, or in a business the CEO or managing director, becomes a resource to the team, not a delegator of tasks.

This single dominant design principle becomes, in turn, an umbrella to others. The four examples below are common to many strategic process patterns increasingly visible in world-class companies:

1. Processes to be driven by customer expectations
2. Maximization of opportunity for interaction between people
3. Decisions to be made by those closest to the work
4. One-time entry of data, accessible to all who need to know

By keeping such organizational principles clearly in focus, managers can weed out poor practices and bring into play others that manifest the guiding principles. They are useful, however, only to the extent that managers and workers know them and can explain what they mean and that the same people actually use them when making decisions. When Procter & Gamble set out to reorganize its worldwide product supply activities in 1992, one of the primary guidelines for the internal design team was that it organize around the process, not the task or function. This allowed the team to downplay the narrow roles and responsibilities traditionally held by functions and to redefine roles only to the extent that they contributed to the successful execution of the global product supply process. "The leverage is in the interrelationships," a Procter & Gamble report observed. The same report concluded that the organization's current structure enhanced functional excellence at the expense of a lack of coordination across departments and functions.

Resistance and organizational inertia can quickly undermine the best of principles. Take, for example, the working principle of maximizing the opportunity for people to interact. These are but words if office doors remain closed (a common European practice) or if executive dining rooms segregate managers from nonmanagers. These are only words, too, if one designs electronic information systems that limit access to a few. Bureaucratic control can interfere. In one French organization employees must fill out forms for permission to spend more than one hour away from their assigned office location and another form to explain what they did, in the event the permission was not issued. In each case the opportunity for interaction is inhibited for real or imagined reasons at the price of constricting any one person's vision of the whole.

Glenn Gardner was one of the individuals who led the Chrysler Corporation's turnaround during the early 1990s. As head of the highly publicized new LH Platform team, which was responsible for designing a new family of car models, Gardner was instrumental in rebuilding the company's product development capabilities, a process that at the time took too long and produced lackluster cars with too many defects. Part of his success was in clearly defining and communicating a family of principles that would guide the way in which work was carried out (see Figure 2.3). The outcome was a flatter organization, co-located work, reliance on specialized competencies (not functions), and a cohesive development program involving suppliers and distributors as integral members of the team. The benefits

2.3. Chrysler's fifteen change principles.

1. Final needs of customer dictate all actions.
2. Quality comes first.
3. Personal goals are second.
4. All non–value-added activity is eliminated.
5. Every employee is empowered to put the customer first (e.g., to take risks).
6. Continuously improve.
7. New timing/scheduling assumptions are made.
8. Suppliers are brought in early and trained.
9. No decision before its time.
10. Value-adding work is on the critical path—not such things as management reviews or approval.
11. Simultaneous engineering and concurrent testing.
12. Decisions pushed to tech level where the information is.
13. Decisions by consensus of all interfaces in the company.
14. Constant focus on who pays for the final product.
15. Benchmark against the best of the best.

Recounted by Glenn Gardner, manager of Chrysler's LH Platform Team, during a presentation to the Product Development Management Association, Atlanta, 1993.

were measured in new car development times of 30 months instead of 45 or more; far fewer engineers on teams, 770 instead of 1400; and substantially lower development costs.

By calling for everyone to act with the whole mission in mind, each can better calibrate and adjust his or her actions reflexively, not through task-specific top-down directives. Such a reflexive and continually self-adjusting ability is central to the vitality and effectiveness of the lean organization. This, of course, is the antithesis of the behavior of managers in the traditional command and control organization where people at the top are always presumed to know best and always like to believe that they do in fact control and contain the rate of change.

❖ A reflexive and continually self-adjusting ability is central to the vitality and effectiveness of the lean organization.

The reflexive company succeeds, especially in complex, fast-moving markets, because it functions as a unified whole. The whole is "centered" when there is not just a sense of *believable* common purpose but, as important, a sense of community that stimulates a feeling that "my contribution will be appreciated." Such conditions allow an organization to adapt quickly to external changes, to better anticipate and provide value to its customers, and to do it by continually stripping away organizational encumbrances. What differentiates it in terms of day-to-day behavior is a keen sensitivity to the quality of interrelationships between people as a driving force. On the other hand, get the values and the patterns of interrelationships wrong and the outcome will never yield a competitive advantage. Get them right and you will win every time, even in times of crises such as those experienced during the rebuilding of Malden Mills.

❖ The reflexive company succeeds, especially in complex, fast-moving markets, because it functions as a unified whole. The whole is "centered" when there is not just a sense of *believable* common purpose but, as important, a sense of community.

34

One company that came to understand the power of similar design principles is Buckman Laboratories International in Memphis, Tennessee, which has 1,200 employees spread across the globe. The CEO, Bob Buckman, has rooted his company's success in its ability to mobilize the full intellectual potential of its workforce. "Over the years, people have taught themselves to hoard knowledge to achieve power," he observed. "We have to reverse that: The most powerful people are those who become a source of knowledge by sharing what they know."[10] Making information easily accessible to every employee is central to Buckman's strategy. Discovering this as a way of doing business occurred to him in 1988 as he recovered from a serious back injury. "The basic philosophy is: How do we take this individual," he remembered thinking to himself, "and make him bigger, give him power? How? Connect him to the world."[11] With this insight he jotted out the principles of a "knowledge transfer system," which would eventually guide the transformation of his company into an upside-down pyramid:

> It would make it possible for people to talk to each other directly, to minimize distortion.
> It would give everyone access to the company's knowledge base.
> It would allow each individual in the company to enter knowledge into the system.
> It would be available twenty-four hours a day, seven days a week.
> It would be easy to use.
> It would communicate in whatever language is best for the user.
> It would be updated automatically, capturing questions and answers as a future knowledge base.[12]

Buckman's ambitions took tangible form in the early 1990s with the creation of global network links. This achievement brought the company his father founded closer to the vision of tapping the whole workforce's intellectual capabilities.

"Intelligence is in the design of the system as well as in people's relationships to a system," observed Mike McMaster, a noted practitioner who has applied complexity theory to the management of organizations.[13] In other words, the most successful organizations are those that act as intelligent organisms able to receive information, interpret it, and translate it quickly and effectively into something of economic value to someone else. This is the operational core of the lean enterprise. It allows the intelligence of the whole workforce to surface unencumbered by artificial barriers.

The design of an "intelligent" process-driven system is the subject of the next chapter. Its defining feature is a three-tier teaming structure.

NOTES

1. David A. Garvin, "Leveraging Processes for Strategic Advantage," *Harvard Business Review* (September–October 1995), p. 77.
2. Ludwig von Bertalanffy, *General Systems Theory* (New York: George Braziller, 1968), p. 5.
3. Peter Senge, *The Fifth Discipline* (New York: Doubleday, 1990), p. 69.
4. Von Bertalanffy, p. 4.
5. Fritjof Capra, *The Web of Life* (New York: Anchor, 1996).
6. Garvin, "Leveraging Processes."
7. James Coplien and Douglas Schmidt, eds., *Pattern Languages of Program Design* (Reading, Mass.: Addison Wesley, 1995), pp. 184–185.
8. Christopher Alexander et al., *A Pattern Language* (New York: Oxford University Press, 1977).
9. Conversations with Dan Dimancescu.
10. Glenn Rifkin, "Nothing But Net," *Fast Company,* June–July 1996.
11. Ibid.
12. Ibid.
13. Michael D. McMaster, *The Intelligence Advantage: Organising for Complexity* (Isle of Man, England: Knowledge Based Development, 1995), p. 49.

Chapter 3

A THREE-TIER SYSTEM

Most decisions are made in isolation; most consequences are systemic.

John Fly, Director of Finance and Corporate Planning, Milliken & Company

In strategic thinking, one first seeks a clear understanding of the particular character of each element of a situation and then makes the fullest possible use of human brain power to restructure the elements in the most advantageous way.

Kenichi Ohmae, *The Mind of the Strategist* (New York: McGraw-Hill, 1982)

C ompeting in today's world of business means adapting to continual and rapid change. "We are now living on Internet time," said Andrew Grove, chief executive of the Intel Corporation, in a June 3, 1996, article by John Markoff in the *New York Times*. The article continued, "His company, which rose to power in an earlier, more measured high-technology pace, is now scrambling to adapt to life at warp speed. 'It's a new territory,' Mr. Grove said, 'and the cyber equivalent of the Oklahoma land rush is on.'" The same article observed, "For a variety of reasons, the Internet has severely compressed the business cycle. . . . Chief among them is the high speed product development that results from exchanging ideas and research over the network." At Sun Microsystems, reported the *Times,* 20 percent of its knowledge is estimated to turn obsolete every year. Time is now talked about in terms of "web-weeks."

This is why so many organizations are shedding a legacy of hierarchical habits which fragmented them into functions and departments. In contrast, lean, adaptable enterprises—large and small—operate with very little bureaucracy and highly sensitive reflexes. Authority in such organizations is being delegated to teams with a minimum of interference from management. This is done by establishing clear performance expectations as well as clear boundaries, much like in a soccer or basketball team, within which members are allowed to act unfettered.

Adapting to change can be so enormous an undertaking, however, that sometimes nothing short of a "radical breakthrough" will work. These were Pierre Blayau's words as the newly appointed CEO of the troubled French giant Moulinex. He said, "The company spends one dollar to earn one dollar in sales. Ten percent of our products lose money. We have three times more suppliers than Renault. We act as though we are a $3 billion company although our actual sales are nearly half that amount. Our losses in 1995 were $300 million. It's a real *waste.* All our competitors perform better and go about their work differently."[1] What are his goals, considering what he inherited? "In three years I want to see per capita sales at $200,000, up from $140,000. In two years our profits will have to go up by 15 percent. I want to be a world-scale company. To do it we need to make a radical breakthrough."[2]

There is a "radical" way of pulling all of the pieces together: a *three-tier system of management* that builds on a lean, three-level hierarchy of senior executive, process, and action teams, each with operational metrics, or benchmarks, tailored to their different roles and responsibilities. The system is constructed on a single overriding design principle discussed in Chapter 2: *The organization must be designed in such a way that the whole can be seen through any of the parts and so that any one part contributes to the whole.* Properly implemented, such an organizational system leads to a workforce with an end-to-end understanding, both of the processes they are involved in and the relevance of the actions they must carry out to meet the organization's business objectives. In short, the three-tier system permits strategy and business objectives to be translated into key processes, and the latter into specific actions.

❖ Properly implemented, such an organizational system leads to a workforce with an end-to-end understanding, both of the processes they are involved in and the relevance of the actions they must carry out to meet the organization's business objectives.

Depicted schematically, the management system consists of three levels of teams: (1) senior management, (2) strategic process owners, and (3) action teams (see Figure 3.1). This tiering method serves to translate top-level (static) objectives, sometimes referred to as the organization's scorecard, into competitively critical (motivational) performance gaps, which, if not narrowed, will diminish an enterprise's competitive vitality, and finally into (dynamic) targeted actions that are executed in short time frames in order to close the gap.

3.1. The three-tier management system.

	Static	**Motivational**	**Dynamic**
Senior Team	Objectives Results		
Process Team		Performance Gaps	
Action Team			Targeted Actions

The term *static* is used because most result measures, such as profitability or market share, have a long lag time between an action and a measured result and thus do not allow corrective action to be taken until too late. *Motivational measures* are so termed because they provide a clear line of sight on the scale of improvement needed, from the customer's perspective, to remain competitive over a five- to ten-year horizon. Dynamic measures, such as control charts, generate real-time data that allow immediate judgments to be made about whether an activity is in or out of control. This allows prompt corrective action to be taken based on an analysis of root causes of the particular problem. Each measurement system provides feedback to the prior level so that the whole system can continually readjust.

To clarify this tiering system one can use the analogy of a nation's Olympics committee. Its expectations and objectives (as an executive team) are measured in medals won—gold, silver, and bronze—and doing so within certain budgetary constraints. One level below are groups focused on particular sports (process teams), such as track, swimming, or cycling. Their job is to design and manage the training process—people, equipment, resources, tools—that will lead to narrowing any gap between their team's current level of performance and the theoretically attainable limits. In track, for example, the 100-meter-dash record is 9.84 seconds. A star athlete does not aim to equal the record but to push beyond to new limits. Assuming the theoretical limit after all variables are calculated is 9.5, and the current capability of a particular nation's best athlete is at 10.03 seconds, the gap to be narrowed is 0.53 seconds. At the next level down (action teams) trainers work on a day-to-day basis with athletes to bring them closer and closer to the theoretical limit. They use dynamic measures to determine calorie intake, hours of training, oxygen usage, and varied other criteria, any of which might yield information that allows immediate corrective actions to be taken. In most sports, because the margins between victory and loss are measured in hundredths of a second, the third-tier dynamic measures are taken very seriously with the aid of new technologies. In sports such as cycling, for example, enormous technical effort is now invested in attempting to shave a single one hundredth of a second of a racer's capability by monitoring aerodynamic flows with computers. The same is true in swimming, skiing, and track. It is no less true in the world of business.

❖ Any individual in this system should be able to see the whole field of play and in this manner mirror its goals at whatever level he or she is working.

The three-tier system, illustrated in Figure 3.1, brings to life the overriding design rule: Any individual in this system should be able to see the whole field of play and in this manner mirror its goals at whatever level he or she is working. Individuals or teams can then better calibrate their actions. Out of this system evolves a structure in which teams and team members with highly specialized competencies are the central actors. Senior managers in such a system set goals and support and coach the teams below. This is the heart of high-performance management, as we will note through the experiences of executives and work teams in the chapters to come.

NEW ROLES AND RESPONSIBILITIES

The role of senior management is to develop the strategic picture and translate it into business goals and objectives. These are then reviewed and readjusted in periodic learning cycles to reflect new external factors or internal events and capabilities. To do this systemically, the senior executive team must be able to identify the vital few core processes needed to meet objectives and to appoint effective teams to design and monitor those processes. Senior management teams are optimal at five to eight members, although it is not uncommon to see the number as high as fifteen. In turn, individuals on the senior team are selected by the CEO to mentor or champion a single strategic process team.

Strategic process teams, designated by senior management and often including members of the senior team, take on the end-to-end and cross-organizational responsibility for managing the quality and effectiveness of a given process, such as order fulfillment or product development. Those processes are described in more detail in Chapter 1. Members of process teams are not assigned full-time. They maintain day-to-day line responsibilities but designate a portion of their time, anywhere from 10 to 30 percent, to oversee the process to which they are delegated. Process-owning teams are required, too, to target and then manage the rate of improvement of critical performance gaps that must be narrowed to remain competitive. A special role played by process teams is to design efficient and effective patterns of cross-organizational relationships and decision making between key players, within and outside the company. These patterns are used as blueprints for teams to follow as a process is executed. Core process teams, in addition, ensure that the resources, equipment, and tool kits of software or training are available for action teams to tap.

Who owns a process? In some cases CEOs designate individuals as the "owners" of key processes. A more effective option is to delegate ownership of a process to the whole team. Performance is thus encouraged by their collective commitment to the process and the effectiveness with which targeted outcomes (performance gap narrowing, for example) is achieved. While the distinction between individual and team ownership of a process is critical to the success of process-minded management, its implications are generally underestimated. When an individual is designated, he or she must be rewarded or recognized in some manner. This not only isolates the owner from the team but works against the more important goal of achieving cross-organizational collaboration. In addition, the individual owner is left with the politically difficult task of continually negotiating the commitment in time and effort of other members of the team, each of whom may be encumbered with other responsibilities and priorities as well as different reward and recognition criteria. Assigning individual accountability for a process runs the risk, too, of returning fast to a functional structure built around individuals rather than a process-focused structure built around cross-organizational teams.

When the team is made fully accountable, there is no question as to the prioritization of individual effort—particularly if the reward and recognition system is designed to gauge the contribution in effort of individuals as team players. Such teams do, of course, have leaders who are selected for their charisma, coaching capability, and judgment. Those leaders serve as the official spokesman, but when an issue arises or a success is acknowledged, it is the team as a whole that is held accountable or given credit.

❖ When the team is made fully accountable, there is no question as to the prioritization of individual effort.

As a result, new names of roles and responsibilities are coming into being to replace formal functional titles (see Figure 3.2). There is, quite naturally, substantial variance in nomenclature between different companies and countries. At American Standard, a global corporation based in New Jersey, there is great pride in the new role of the process coach, whose responsibility it is to nurture the capabilities of process team members. At Mitel, a Canadian communication systems business, its British subsidiary interprets the concept of a coach very differently but just as dynamically, as discussed in Chapter 7.

The last group of teams in the three-tier system are the action teams. This is where the rubber hits the road. Their role is to narrow critical performance gaps by brainstorming and prioritizing actions that can be taken, then carrying them out. This kind of teamwork is now widespread in world-class companies that compete on the basis of fast and effective performance. Innovative methods in teaming at low levels in the organization were first applied more than two decades ago at the shop-floor level and were termed *work cells*. Workers said they found it much easier and intuitively right to work in this manner. Successes at this level helped eradicate a Tayloristic legacy of union titles and narrowly prescribed job specifications. It is only more recently that this learning has migrated, and with much more difficulty, higher up into the managerial and executive levels of organizations. Spoiled by a long tradition of rewards and perks aimed at individual achievement, managers and executives are often highly resistant to anything that smacks of true teamsmanship, as much as they may use the rhetoric.

3.2. New organizational roles and responsibilities.

First tier	Process strategists	Establishes executive direction and priorities and monitors results
	Process champion	Shepherds process owners and provides counsel and guidance
Second tier	Process owner(s)	Accountable for the quality of the execution of a core process
	Process coach	Provides support to team and human resource assistance
Third tier	Team leaders	Brings focus and guidance to shared activities
	Members	Brings specific competency and skills to an action-focused team
Support	Competency champion	Ensures support for maintaining center of excellence capabilities and monitors those capabilities
	Competency owner	Maintains center of excellence focused on maintaining the highest possible level of achievement in core competencies

❖ With the three-tier system comes a transformation of traditional functional roles—such as engineering or manufacturing or marketing—into competencies.

With the three-tier system comes a transformation of traditional functional roles—such as engineering, manufacturing, and marketing—into competencies, or specialized capabilities that contribute value-adding knowledge to a company and so in turn to its customers. In a software company, for example, the vital competence may be in a particular software language; at an automobile manufacturer it may be a profound understanding of new materials such as plastic polymers; and at a fast-food chain the critical competence may be in logistics. These individual competencies are pooled in process and action teams. Leading companies are "housing" these capabilities not under old functional labels but in "Competency Centers" as at Chrysler in Michigan, or "Centers of Excellence" as at Sabre Development Systems in Oklahoma.

A TRANSFER OF POWER

If there is unease with all this "process stuff" in managerial ranks, it is because of a perception that traditional corporate power bases are being undermined. At Hewlett-Packard, a leader in instituting a process-based management system, it is acknowledged that a fundamental transfer of power is at play. "A growing number of levers of process authority," states a 1995 internal document (used by permission), are drawing substantial decision-making power and budgetary control away from the more traditional functional structure. The latter, in the words of the report, are evolving into "discipline or competence centers of excellence" necessary to support key processes. These centers nurture and develop core skills that are critical to the competitive advantage of the company.

❖ If there is unease with all this "process stuff" in managerial ranks, it is because of a perception that traditional corporate power bases are being undermined.

Characteristics of the power shift at Hewlett-Packard away from functional to process team control include:

- Controlling the (re)design of the process
- Sitting at the right hand of the CEO
- Setting process measures
- Linking process measures to contingent compensation
- Negotiating service-level contracts
- Conducting budgeting by process
- Controlling the "change program" budget

- Controlling key process aspects
- Controlling strategic planning for the process

Responsibilities such as these and the transfer of power associated with them mark a radical transition to a new style of management behavior. This transition to a process-driven strategy may be as fundamental as the century-old invention of scientific management by Frederick Winslow Taylor and contemporaries of his such as Gantt and Fayol. Their pioneering work was further refined by numerous others, and later by the American quality trio of W. Edwards Deming, Joseph Juran, and Dr. A. V. Feigenbaum and their Japanese disciples, such as Dr. Kaoru Ishikawa, Taiichi Ohno, and professor and Dr. Genichi Taguchi.

Although their contributions revolutionized an industrial world based on machine-assisted manual work, the contemporary world is based only in small part on traditional machine-based work. These same individuals have had far less influence on the knowledge-intensive or service-intensive sectors, in which intangibles such as information and non–machine-based activity breed competitive advantage. In today's world, it is the ability of companies to manage resources such as intellect, knowledge, and information that distinguish the winners from the losers. Hence, the need for a radical shift. Indeed, one can watch with both amusement and dismay attempts by very sophisticated managers to apply generic total quality management practices—based on learning that matured in mass production assembly plants—in business sectors where knowledge is the principle ingredient transacted and sold. Diminishing returns quickly set in.

❖ This transition to a process-driven strategy may be as fundamental as the century-old invention of scientific management by Frederick Winslow Taylor.

At Hewlett-Packard the question of whether the word *management* may not itself be obsolete is now asked. One reason is the realization that process "performers" do not behave like "workers."

Rather than their blind observance of a task, it is their ability to make informed judgments that is valued. It is just such an ability that defies conventional application of manufacturing-generated quality tools intended at their origin to master "machine systems"—thus the underlying principles embedded in statistical process control, a concept applicable to a world of machines, the behavior of which can be quantified and controlled. Hewlett-Packard's insight conforms to author Mike McMaster's compelling definition of an intelligent organization. He suggests that "guidance is by patterns rather than detail—the guidance is directional rather than absolute."[3] In other words, given the right compass setting, resources, and training, process teams will determine how best to get there. This is what sets the three-tier system apart from a management system executed by rigidly prescribed three-ring binder rulebooks and narrowly prescribed tasks. In its stead a new kind of behavior is taking hold.

NOTES

1. "Du passé de Moulinex, Pierre Blayau veut faire table rase," *Le Nouvelle Economiste,* no. 1053, June 21, 1996.
2. Ibid.
3. Michael D. McMaster, *The Intelligence Advantage: Organising for Complexity* (Isle of Man, England: Knowledge Based Development, 1995).

Chapter 4

NONLINEAR TEAMING

*A lot of nature is nonlinear—including most of what's really in-
teresting in the world. Our brains certainly aren't linear: even
though the sound of an oboe and the sound of a string section may
be independent when they enter your ear, the emotional impact of
both sounds may be very much greater than either one alone.
(This is what keeps symphony orchestras in business.)*

        M. Mitchell Waldrop, *Complexity* (New York: Simon
        and Schuster, 1992)

*The linear language, which we have inherited both socially and
for business affairs, does not allow for emergent phenomena or
complex systems; it therefore leaves us powerless when dealing
with such things. Those who have developed the understanding
and vocabulary of complex systems can see certain things that are
invisible to others. Thus, they have a greater range of action,
possibility and power available to them.*

        Michael D. McMaster, *The Intelligence Advantage:
        Organising for Complexity* (Isle of Man: Knowledge Based
        Development, 1995)

W hat distinguishes the three-tier teaming system from a functionally fragmented one is the way in which individuals interact and perform their work. At one extreme is the task-based functional organization. At the other is the three-tier teaming system that puts far more emphasis on the quality of working relationships between people as a competitive resource. The distinction between the two is so significant that it marks both a new understanding of complex organizations and a radical change in management philosophy. As illustrated in Figure 4.1, the former relies on precise job descriptions and top-down directives to make it work. Individuals in this case have no control over the process within which they work and most often very little knowledge of the workings of the whole process. The second is based on trusting groups of people to manage their own interrelationships and delegating to them control from beginning to end over the whole process, for which they are then held accountable.

In a task-based environment, communication is through a formal chain of authority, generally sequential in nature. For a message to reach someone elsewhere in an organization, it must travel up a ladder of control and down again. Everything is based on permission and procedure and centralized management of information. Orders and work methods are directed from the top, never from the bottom, and then filter downward through layers of middle managers and

4.1. Task-based vs. relationship-based management.

Linear	**Nonlinear**
Task-based with supervisors (interactions are controlled)	Relationship-based teams with a leader (everyone is free to interact with anyone else)

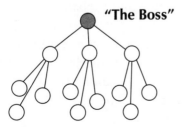

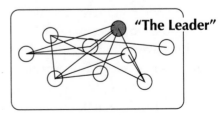

supervisors. Little is left to judgment. Some companies, such as Mc-
Donald's, succeed for the very simple reason that they leave little to
the judgment of individuals working at a local retail store. An operation such as this, linear as it is (that is, follow step one, then go to
step two, and so on), may work in some environments requiring
strict control for whatever reason, but its effectiveness diminishes
rapidly in situations that are knowledge intensive and require fast,
flexible reactions.

This is why relationship-based management—a defining feature
of a process-driven organization—is so different. Its defining quality
is that tasks are not dictated and communication is nonlinear. One of
its strengths is that, as author Roger Lewin wrote, "small inputs can
lead to dramatically large consequences."[1] But, as Lewin points out,
although the system may behave predictably most of the time, you
never quite know when or what new outcome there might be. The
best one can do is keep people moving toward a common destination and then get out of the way. Silicon Valley is a good example of
an economy driven by nonlinear relationships. In such a freewheel-
ing technological environment, the real creative force is that anybody can talk to anybody else when and if they wish, no matter what
company they work for. "In the Valley, direction comes from loyalty
to the technology," locals will say, not to the employer. This is one
reason why news and ideas travel so fast. One talks shop anywhere
at anytime, and one never quite knows where or when the next
breakthrough will occur. Such unpredictability keeps venture capi-
talists busy trolling for opportunities.

In today's world the most pervasive form of nonlinear interaction has exploded into life with the Internet. Its principal quality is
in unfettered communication between anyone, anytime, anywhere.
From it are emerging new forms of interaction and exchange—such
as electronic commerce or virtual problem solving between individuals who have never met—that are generating new but as yet unde-
fined behaviors and organizational forms. Of the many thousands of
examples is an electronic forum centered on the Learning Organization as a shared topic, an interest coordinated by Professor Peter M.
Senge at the Massachusetts Institute of Technology in Cambridge,

Massachusetts. About 150 intellectuals are frequent contributors through written messages, and about 2,000 other individuals enter and exit periodically merely to scan the ongoing dialogue. The interaction and the learning transferred is nonlinear. It is not orchestrated, nor is any part of it required to be sequential, although some pieces of the dialogue may appear so. Leading organizations are learning to tap such unstructured exchanges and turn them into a knowledge-creating competitive resource.

Social settings such as restaurants and bars have always served as nonlinear meeting places. In European and Japanese culture, these have been vital points of nonlinear interaction that make up for the rigidities present in the workplace. This is where chance encounters occur, information is often exchanged among strangers, new ideas germinate over sketches on napkins. Such nonlinearity is not possible in a disciplined, task-based corporate setting, because considerable power can be had by hoarding information and preventing access to it. Overcoming such obstructions calls for a different kind of behavior that encourages individuals to freely initiate and exchange ideas and to explore new concepts.

At companies such as Otikon in Denmark, Mitel in Wales, and Astra Hässle Laboratories in Sweden, offices and laboratories are designed to include social meeting places where chance encounters can occur and two to five people can relax and discuss ideas over coffee. Old pyramid-like organization charts are abandoned; titles are out. At Otikon, reported a business magazine, "projects, not functions or departments became the defining unit of work."[2] The article's subtitle reads "No Titles. No Offices. No Paper. How Denmark's Otikon Thrives on Chaos."

"By organizing work around teams," said the CEO Lars Kolind, "we want each project to feel like a company, and the project leader to feel like a CEO. We allow a lot of freedom." Commercial creativity is seen as a by-product of maximum freedom of communication. Because there is no such thing as a permanent office at Otikon, individuals actually roll their moveable offices about in order to be close to the appropriate project teams. In a comment that would appear anarchic to a traditionalist, Kolind said, "to keep a company alive, one of the jobs of top-management is to keep it dis-orga-nized." The key, of course, is to guide the pattern of change in such a way that the whole grows healthier as it adapts. This is the critical role played by someone like Kolind.

❖ To keep a company alive, one of the jobs of top-manage-ment is to keep it dis-organized.

In a world of complex systems this type of behavior is referred to as generative because out of it come new ideas that cause structural changes to occur. And for every change, the system is permanently altered in some way, visible or not. Some might call this a Darwinian form of evolution; others might call it living in a state of continual disequilibrium, or what has been characterized as living on the edge of chaos. Whatever the choice, what is unassailable is that companies, and cultures, that wither, other than those that are victim to incom-petence, are those that fail to develop adaptive mechanisms. Among these have been many well-known companies such as Penn Central, Pan Am, Howard Johnson's British Leyland, and Fokker.

Because knowledge has economic value, the productive role of nonlinear interactions is now understood by more and more compa-nies. Even in the cloistered world of government defense contracts, where stifling bureaucratic constraints led to the institutionalization of task-based matrix management, new rules are swamping out old ones as cost pressures and declining markets force radical change. When a team of managers at Pilkington Optronics, a Welsh manu-facturer of defense optical components for aircraft, tanks, and subma-rines, met to brainstorm about radical structural changes in the defense world, they concluded that freeing work teams to control their own actions was a survival measure. This would allow more nimble response to contractual opportunities and more effective exe-cution under stringent cost constraints. A well-defined common aim is the real boundary around a team. But within the boundary, they agreed, there should be little or no formal reporting. Although they might have been reluctant to call this nonlinear behavior, that is what it was. The working principle is to minimize external management interference while maximizing internal team freedom to act.

❖ The working principle is to minimize external management interference while maximizing internal team freedom to act.

Architecture can itself highlight the contrast in task- and relationship-based management. This became evident when Hyperion Software moved its 1,100 employees into the plush headquarters of the old-line Combustion Engineering in Stamford, Connecticut. The vacated headquarters, sold at a bargain price, had been designed for a traditional hierarchical culture marked by lavish executive offices with fireplaces and private kitchens. Into this space moved a nonlinear culture of software developers for whom titles and posh decors had little relevance or meaning. "The softly gleaming boardroom," reported a newspaper story, "and a chairman's office with working fireplace and antique French marble is now home to Hyperion's training center for its customers' employees." Of greater importance to the software company, however, is a "floor plan that encourages people working in teams to shout across a room or to walk across. . . . The point is to avoid impeding the creative flow with dress codes, fixed schedules or unnecessary walls."[3]

Similar intentions are in growing evidence in other institutions. When the School of Management at Boston University inaugurated its new home in October 1996, the $100 million building showcased one critical architectural feature: glassed offices and corridors that exposed faculty, students, and administrators to one another independent of their departmental titles. The unabashed intent, encouraged by the School's dean, Lou Lataif, was to induce informal interactions and thus opportunities for innovation.

Dean Lataif states his vision of this new open environment as follows:

> We were determined to take advantage of this once-in-a-century opportunity to configure our new building to impact positively the inter-

53

actions of people in it. Consequently, all our faculty offices are located on two floors—intermixed by academic discipline. Coffee rooms are interspersed among the offices to further encourage interaction. A separate open stairwell was added to the middle of the building to foster maximum communication between the faculty floors. Faculty and staff offices are glass-walled to bring natural light to virtually all offices but, more importantly, to again encourage contact and interaction.

ALIGNING THE THREE-TIER SYSTEM

The three-tier hierarchy of teams, lean in layers, helps minimize the role of any reporting bureaucracy and, in this manner, opens the door to greater interaction between people. It also allows more complex problems to be tackled by teams rather than be delegated as tasks to individuals working less effectively at arm's length. For this system of management to work effectively, however, teams must be given clear objectives and precisely defined constraints within which they can then be empowered to work unfettered by management interference. This allows teams themselves the latitude to determine how best to execute the required action.

❖ For this system of management to work effectively, however, teams must be given clear objectives and precisely defined constraints within which they can then be empowered to work unfettered by management interference.

Actions need to be focused and calibrated. Hence the importance of building a system of metrics, or benchmarks, that translates top-level objectives into actions that will aggregate into a whole. This approach varies significantly from a task-driven culture, where the manner in which a task is to be performed is more important than its purpose or objective. The effect is to minimize any latitude of judgment on how the task is carried out. Workers are thus disenfranchised. In a knowledge-intensive working environment this is a recipe for failure.

"Metrics," writes Arthur Schneiderman, originator in the late

1980s of the scorecard concept, when he served as a vice-president of Analog Devices, "are measures you can manage against."[4] Hence the need to take scorecard-style business objectives, which are static and therefore harder to manage against, and translate them into process-focused performance gaps. Described in more detail in Chapter 5, these can be managed by breaking them down into prioritized and well-targeted actions. These actions are controlled, in turn, by applying real-time measures indicating whether day-to-day or week-to-week progress is proceeding as planned.

When first introduced to this three-tier system, executives and managers are skeptical about the benefits. One reason is that the system fits poorly within a "big company" structure in which power and authority is functionally based. In such cases few executives or managers can match traditional career expectations or their day-to-day responsibilities to the expected new behavior. Yet, when given time to deliberate and to free themselves of preconceived organizational notions, they are quick to acknowledge the value of team accountability for managing complex processes such as product development or order fulfillment. The shortcomings of functional departments soon become apparent. Once grasped, this insight can then be transferred by the executive team to process teams and later to action teams.

With such realizations comes a slow, often painful, learning cycle that is many times ignored in corporate reengineering efforts aimed at introducing a process-driven system. "An essential ingredient," according to Peter Russell and Roger Evans, British experts on the psychology and dynamics of change management, "is to foster the individual's own creative processes; that is, to help them understand their own inner worlds, trust themselves and their insights, communicate what they truly feel, see their own mind-sets and step back from them, be aware of their own hidden motivations, and, perhaps most important *if we are all to pull together,* be in touch with their hearts and their sense of what truly matters."[5] From such insight flows a sense of empowerment that will, in turn, breed confidence. It helps answer a growing need for meaningful connections to people and the organization within which one works. Building inner confidence is an essential step in moving away from an insular work environment governed by narrowly prescribed tasks to one in which collaborative behavior is valued as the modus operandi.

For consultant on creative learning Alex Pattakos, a deeper social force is at work. "As workers at all levels in organizational hierarchies experience a sense of disconnectedness from one another in the pursuit of the 'bottom line,' a yearning has developed among the populations of companies and other work places. This yearning originates from a need to feel a part of a community. This fundamental human need to feel connected to others is driving good people out of organizations or, worse yet, into unhealthy lifestyles should they resign themselves to endure the separations they find at work."[6]

The three-tier system, based on a holistic view of an enterprise and a team-based structure, is one answer to this thirst for connectedness. This yearning is experienced in teaming work sessions—particularly at the action level—that brainstorm actions that affect a customer need and in turn a companywide objective. The sense of connectedness to both purpose and to a larger whole among workers and managers is tangible and motivating. An example occurred at one of the Trane's air conditioning equipment plants in Trenton, New Jersey, after twenty-five plant workers spent a full day translating a performance gap into tangible actions. "You know something," said a shop-floor employee, "I've never felt that I had any effect on what was going on in the company. After what we did today I can see it and it makes a hell of a difference."

Why is this sense of connectedness necessary? In many industries success requires fast responses to change, an ability to assimilate information rapidly and translate it into something of value to a customer, and above all to achieve consistency of performance over time. These are conditions that a task-based management system has greater and greater difficulty delivering. The lean organization with a three-tier, process-driven system is far better positioned to delegate and adjust because critical information can be assimilated and reacted to, not on a piecemeal basis, but in the context of companywide goals. This is an essential step in arriving at a whole that is greater than the sum of its parts. A daunting challenge, however, is in pacing the rate of change in order to stay abreast of competitors and preferably ahead of them.

NOTES

1. Roger Lewin, *Complexity: Life on the Edge of Chaos* (New York: Macmillan, 1993).
2. Polly Labarre, "This Organization Is Disorganization," *Fast Company,* June–July 1996, special insert.
3. George Judson, "Pampering Those Who Dream Up the Software," *New York Times,* May 17, 1996, p. B6.
4. Conversation with Dan Dimancescu.
5. Peter Russell and Roger Evans, *The Creative Manager* (San Francisco: Jossey-Bass, 1992), p. 157.
6. Alex Pattakos, comments about *Community Building: Renewing Spirit and Learning in Business,* edited by Scott Peck (Boise, Idaho: Creative Learning Technologies, 1995).

Chapter 5

MANAGING THE RATE
OF CHANGE

If you don't measure it, it will not improve. If you don't monitor it, it will get worse.

Arthur Schneiderman, former vice-president of quality at Analog Devices

It has been understood that anyone who announces a program beginning with the word "Toward . . ." probably does not intend to get anywhere. People will not get on an airplane whose flight plan calls for it to fly "toward" New York. Nor will those who intend to get a solution abide by a program that merely aims "toward" the goal.

John Gall, *Systemantics: How Systems Really Work and How They Fail* (Ann Arbor, Mich.: General Systemantics Press, 1986)

I n a process-focused company, business objectives—or what is frequently called the scorecard—contain more than simple financial goals. Such things as profitability, revenue targets, or return on net assets are unavoidably important, but two other categories complement them. One group addresses customer objectives generally expressed in quality, cost, or delivery metrics; another focuses on employees by establishing morale, training, and safety goals. In this way the enterprise acknowledges the equal importance of its key constituents—shareholders, customers, and employees.

Yet the seemingly simple translation of top-level business objectives into actions remains problematic in many companies, as the following vignette suggests.

The senior management team of a billion-dollar corporate division was gathered at a plush Texas golf club for a two-day work session. Sitting in a horseshoe pattern in a darkly paneled room, the twelve senior managers awaited a discussion with their newly appointed executive vice-president. The parent company had recently gone public after a painful and costly leveraged buyout that stripped cash resources out of operations to pay for high interest on its debt. Accelerated rates of growth and profitability were now expected of its divisions, in a market requiring more stringent quality standards and price competition. Hence the meeting to discuss the consequences.

"Gentlemen," the executive vice-president opened, "all of you received the seven objectives I issued for our business. Our agenda today is to discuss how to deploy them more effectively down into your organizations." Even though the ensuing deliberations continued over two days, the most telling lesson came early. It had to do with the business's objectives and an assumption, falsely held as it turned out, that they were crystal clear to everyone present. For example, one business objective called for a 50 percent improvement in quality in three years. But it soon became evident that there was no firm definition of quality nor a numerical basis for measuring it. Even after one was found, two major business units, one focused on industrial accounts and another on residential sales, could not agree on the proportion of the improvement they should be held accountable to deliver. To further confuse matters, the time frame for achieving the improvement became hazier and hazier as the conversation wore on. Three years was mentioned by the divisional head, but no one could agree on when those three years would begin: Was it the calendar year or the July 1 fiscal year? Was it as of today, the day of the meeting? A six-month difference could have enormous implications if one's bonus depended on it.

Failed communication on matters as basic as this is widespread but, strangely enough, rarely treated by senior managers as a serious shortcoming. Good managers can generally muddle their way to success. To an outside observer, however, such a case is evidence of an organization in which actions will be fragmented. If fourteen managers leave the room with fourteen different opinions on what is expected of them, how can anyone else in the company be expected to act with the whole organization's interest in mind? They simply can't. Under such circumstances, management teams cannot effectively align their own objectives, much less those of persons reporting to them. Inevitably, some months later anger will flare when poorly communicated expectations are not met. If the CEO is clever, someone else will take the blame.

There is a better way of turning business objectives into a coherent set of actions that equal a greater whole. Speaking of the system he put into practice, Arthur Schneiderman, former vice-president for quality at Analog Devices (a maker of semiconductors in Massachusetts), who pioneered the scorecard concept[1] and process-based metrics, recalled:

> An entire system of . . . metrics was incorporated in an on-line executive information system used for management of the scorecard. By pointing and clicking on this entry, the order fulfillment metrics [for example] appeared, now disaggregated by division, credit, warehouse, and customer. Clicking on any number displayed its time history. By clicking on a metric its disaggregation appeared. The system allowed drill-down to the level of individual customers (about 400).

> A manager using this system could, within minutes, determine the levels and trends in performance by division or major customer and could assess whether performance was being improved suboptimally, for example, by trading off delivery performance against lead-time.

> The most insightful display was generated by clicking on an entity's half-life. This produced a time-history of the twelve month running

average. This was the principal indicator of the "double loop" learning with respect to the improvement process.[2] A declining half-life [curve] was a clear indication of the entity's increased mastery of the improvement process.[3]

A well-crafted scorecard, reviewed quarterly by a management team and adjusted annually, expresses a company's strategic direction in quantifiable terms. Scorecard objectives might include:

- Earnings before income and tax
- Return on net assets
- Gross sales
- Market share (by product lines)
- Quality ratings
- Price-to-product performance ratios
- Delivery performance
- Defect rates on critical products or components
- Health and safety ratios per employee (accidents, absenteeism, turnover)
- Employee satisfaction ratings

A similar approach, used by companies such as AT&T, is built on indexed objectives for each of the constituent categories. These indices, treated as business targets, go under the labels of economic value added (EVA) for shareholders, customer value added (CVA) for customers, and personnel value added (PVA) for employees. The indices are compared to best-in-class benchmarks, and target values are set as objectives. The current CVA might be rated at a 1.08, for example, against a best-in-class benchmark of 1.20 and a target objective of 1.30.

The problem of deployment is not resolved by having well-crafted or unambiguous measures in a business scorecard. The reality is that these numbers are generally of very little interest or have little meaning to individuals at lower levels of an organization. Few employees can generate any emotional excitement about improving a company's return on assets. Rare is the worker who might see a direct connection between his or her labor and something as remote as assets or a return on them. Sales growth expectations are another example. What is being designed today may not reach the market for two or three years. There is, as a result, little direct connection between the day-to-day work of a product designer and the business objective of increasing sales volume. Greater efficiency calls for better ways of bridging the chasm between goals and actions. It is critical to achieving the flexibility and speed of adaptation associated with a lean enterprise.

❖ The problem is not resolved by having well-crafted or unambiguous measures in a business scorecard. The reality is that these numbers are generally of very little interest or have little meaning to individuals at lower levels of an organization.

According to John Fly of Milliken & Company: "When we have people working cross-functionally to achieve targeted objectives using a reliable method for doing the work, then we have cross-functional organization. Otherwise, we have only cross-functional activity."[4] This relationship between objective and value adding work can be displayed in a simple matrix showing objectives on one axis and processes on another (see Figure 5.1). At any one intersection point between an objective and a core process, the impact the process will have on the objective can be rated either high, medium, or low.

In Figure 5.1, process C is judged to have a high impact on objectives 2 and 5. This helps clarify the outcomes expected of the members of process team C. Because there is little expectation of an effect on objectives 4 and 6, rated as low, one is forced right away to look to another process for an impact on that objective. Such an exercise allows the organization's executive team to deliberate and visualize the dynamics of the "whole" business. It can therefore better strategize its competitive advantage from a process perspective.

More importantly, the matrix sets the stage for brainstorming

5.1. Strategic process matrix.

Objective	Process A	Process B	Process C	Process D	Process E
1			◯		
2			●		
3			◯		
4			△		
5			●		
6			△		

● High Impact

◯ Medium Impact

△ Low Impact

performance gaps that must be narrowed by each of the process-owning teams in order to meet the business's objectives. The operational responsibility of closing these gaps is delegated, in turn, to action teams. This cascading three-tier procedure is carried out and reviewed annually or biannually by the senior executive team as a Plan Do Check Act (PDCA) cycle.

Much like a ship at sea, a core process must not only be steered toward a fixed goal, but its progress must be measured at regular intervals. Well-defined performance gaps fill the roles of defining a specific destination and charting progress in getting there. To do this, several sources of data are needed by a core process team: a studied understanding of what value is expected by customers, the historic trend lines reflecting how the company has responded to these expectations, and industry or competitor data on meeting the same needs. Because they focus attention on real and immediate actions that can be taken, these curves are a vital and highly motivational bridge between business objectives and meaningful actions. This can be attributed, too, to the customer orientation of the performance metric. Ken Compton of Milliken & Company is adamant in his belief that "a barrier to collaboration is having the wrong measures. You must go beyond the scope of each individual function by getting the right measures . . . and these are defined by customer needs."

Use of performance gaps to manage the rate of change is exemplified by the aluminum can industry, for which the competition is from steel, plastic, and glass container materials. To remain competitive the industry has had to sustain consistent performance improvements for more than thirty years. The critical variable in this case is weight, because beverage producers have little interest in incurring additional shipping cost by lugging heavy containers. In addition, less weight equals substantially lower costs, given the high cost of energy in making aluminum. In 1963, when aluminum first became an accepted material for beer and soda containers, technology permitted a weight of about 0.66 ounces. Thirty years later the weight was reduced to 0.48 ounces, and production exceeded 100 billion cans a year, with steel having been almost eliminated as an alternative material in the North American market (but not in the United Kingdom, where it remains a preferred material). Manufacturers know that the weight of the aluminum can must be reduced to 0.33 ounces by the year 2005 to survive as a preferred material in the container industry. The simplified performance curve in Figure 5.2 shows steep improvement leveling off as improvements get harder and harder to achieve. Translated into logarithmic terms, the curves become a straight line.

Any core-process-owning team can identify at least one customer-sensitive performance gap, probably two or three, that, if

5.2. Reducing the weight of aluminum containers: declining rate of success.

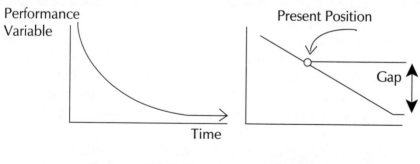

Performance Variable

Time

Exponential Curve

Present Position

Gap

Logarithmic Version

narrowed at the appropriate rate, will lead to meeting business objectives. In the semiconductor industry, for example, Gordon Moore, cofounder of Intel in 1968, observed prophetically several years later that the number of semiconductors put on a chip would double every year. Even more surprising were the economic consequences. "Because the doublings in density were not accompanied by an increase in cost, the expense per transistor was halved with each doubling," according to an article in *Scientific American*.[5] Plotted on a thirty-year performance curve, memory increased exponentially from one thousand transistors per chip in 1971, to 256,000 by 1985, to 16 million by 1995, and to a projected capability of 256 million by the year 2000. Managing the rate of change was a key to Intel's dazzling string of successes over several decades. In the case of Yokogawa-Hewlett-Packard in Japan, one quality metric played a critical role in driving it to sustain world-class performance capability. This was the measure of soldering defects of leads from a chip onto a computer board. In 1970, they were measured in parts per thousand; by 1980, in parts per million; by 1990, in parts per billion. Few doubt that the number will soon reach parts per trillion.

"The first requirement for a good metric," according to Schneiderman, "is that it be a reliable proxy for customer (or stakeholder) satisfaction. In other words, improvement in the metric should link directly to improved customer satisfaction. This linkage should be clear and uncomplicated. It should be single-valued, or 'monotonic,' that is, improvement in the metric should always produce improved customer satisfaction. There should be no optimum value for the metric."[6]

❖ The first requirement for a good metric is that it be a reliable proxy for customer (or stakeholder) satisfaction. In other words, improvement in the metric should link directly to improved customer satisfaction.

Assuming that the correct process metric is selected, two curves must be drawn, one showing your company's performance over an extended period and the other a key competitor's performance. In the event your company is the superior performer, the improvement rate of your closest competitors will have to be closely tracked to ensure that your lead is not being narrowed. Once this is done, the process team must calculate the theoretical limit of the core process based on known technology. This establishes a realistic goal to aim for five to ten years forward. In the communications industry, for example, a dramatic performance battle is in play between twisted copper wires (telephone companies), optical cables (cable companies), and satellites (global telecommunication providers), each vying to deliver the biggest chunks of Internet bandwidth at the lowest possible cost to home and business users.

Copper, the dominant telephone wiring medium through which electrons travel back and forth, might easily be perceived as a has-been technology against optical cables that move photons at the speed of light. In fact, direct voice calls plus data transfer through modems use a startlingly low one half of one percent of present-day copper wire capacity. Ready to tap into the remaining 99.5 percent unused capacity is a new technology—asymmetrical digital subscriber line (ADSL) modems—that can move bits through the same copper cable at least 100 times faster and potentially 300 times faster. What this means, as shown in Figure 5.3, is a performance gap for copper wires between today's potential of 14,400 to 128,000 bits per second (bps) and a demonstrated six million bps with current ADSL to a potential ADSL performance at 18 million bps. Theoretical limits with VDSL (very high speed ADSL) are already known to be five to six times as high as those numbers. Because competitive optical cable is currently able to operate at 10 million bps, one can quickly see the potential for copper and the dimension of the battleground when drawn as performance gaps.

If your business was optical cable modem (bottom of the left row) and your current performance was 10 megabits per second, how fast would you have to push your speed performance (and cost) to stay ahead of copper? Alternatively, if you were copper-focused, would you not want to know the trend line for competing optical cable modems and the rate of change as it reaches its theoretical

5.3. Ever faster: Internet access speeds.

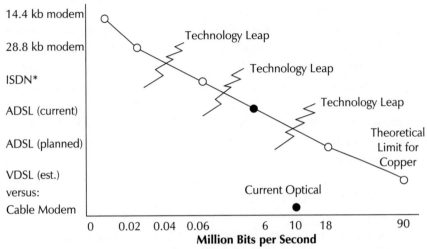

*ISDN (Integrated Services Digital Network) works at 64 kb and can be doubled to 128 kb.

limits? If one supplies products to this market, the answers would be vital to managing key companywide processes that "own" the responsibility to progress down those curves, such as product development and order fulfillment. For Analog Devices, a provider of semiconductor chips that are the most expensive component of an ADSL modem, its trend lines indicate a decline in price of this class of chips by half every eighteen months. Hence, there is a realistic expectation of what it will take to be price competitive. Such numbers are the drivers that motivate process-owning teams.

Targeting performance toward a theoretical limit is far superior to establishing benchmarks based on current knowledge of competitors' capabilities. Although the latter is valuable, it does not account for the fact that the competitor is undoubtedly moving forward to a new level of performance—or the speed with which it may be doing so. A process team must focus outer limits set by the technology, not by the current benchmark.

❖ Targeting performance toward a theoretical limit is far superior to establishing benchmarks based on current knowledge of competitors' capabilities.

This approach allows a process team to better strategize the type and rate of improvement. Two basic choices then present themselves: (1) to invest in a breakthrough in order to radically reshape the direction of the curve or (2) to maintain a consistent and continuous rate of improvement. In Figure 5.4, which shows a competitor's (logarithmic) trend line quickly outpacing the company in question, there is no choice but to attempt a breakthrough because continued progress on the current performance curve would lead the company further and further away from the competitor's superior rate of improvement.

STRATEGIC CHOICES

One form of process innovation can be termed breakthrough management; another is a commitment to continuous improvement. Traditionally, Western companies have tended toward breakthrough management, typically involving the introduction of new enabling technology such as MRP or SAP systems or software such as the CATIA 3D system used by Boeing to automate the design of its new 777 aircraft. Both approaches have advantages and limitations. These efforts carry a risk, however, of optimizing performance in one functional area while undermining end-to-end performance of the whole process. A problem, too, is that a breakthrough lasts only until a

5.4. Keeping pace with the competitor.

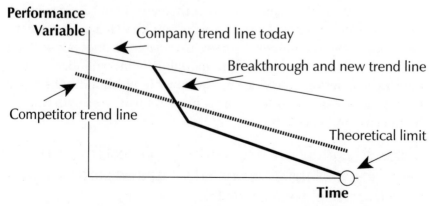

competitor purchases or emulates the innovation employed. At the same time, continuous improvement has a decay curve requiring steady infusions of resources and effort to achieve seemingly smaller competitive gains. In Western firms, continuous improvement teams have a tendency to drift aimlessly out of control after a period of time. Success is generally linked to consistent CEO pressure, such as that from George Fisher at Motorola, whose leadership sustained aggressive improvement rates over an extended period of years.

Many companies create business plans specifying the need for price competitiveness of existing and new products within the markets they serve. The strategic process team then translates the directional thrust of the business plan into more concrete and competitive terms. The results of this activity and the competitive market analysis behind it might lead to the conclusion that an existing product family needs to have a cost reduction of 25 percent in order to realize a market price decrease of 10 percent. New products must therefore be priced competitively while protecting margins and the recovery of associated R&D costs. Faced with such a challenge, the team of managers assess the costs that need to be saved in their respective departments. Inhibitors are identified. From this point, the appropriate improvement activity can be targeted and acted on between departments.

This type of analysis is just what the automobile parts maker Nippondenso carried out in Japan, according to an article in *Sloan Management Review.* "In setting targets for the radiator design, the Nippondenso team graphed performance-to-weight ratios of radiators built during the past several decades. They then projected this data and set targets to beat the competition in the next decade, which required a 50 percent reduction in radiator weight."[7] This was a strategy followed very successfully, too, by Llanelli Radiators in Wales, now a division of Calsonic. In 1990, with only 2 percent of the European market, the company faced extinction because its performance curves in quality, cost, and delivery were all showing insufficient improvement rates. However, a capital infusion from its new owner, Calsonic, allowed the company to strategize a breakthrough in technology by introducing automated brazed aluminum to its production lines. This allowed high labor costs from manual procedures to decline sharply, heat transfer characteristics to increase, and weight to be reduced—all critical performance curves driven by the needs of the automotive industry. Within a few short years, Calsonic Llanelli Radiators captured 16 percent of the market and anticipated higher percentages in the future.

Similar choices confronted Procter & Gamble in 1991 when its research revealed competitors improving their cost structure at a more rapid rate. Probing the causes, an internal study team concluded, much to its surprise, that Procter & Gamble did not have the "organizational capacity" to catch up. The conclusion: An organizational breakthrough was needed to change the slope of its performance curve. This is exactly what the group's executive vice-president set out to do within the far-flung Global Product Supply Group. Over the ensuing two years, a team of fourteen line managers was empowered to redesign the management of its global supply chain along horizontal process lines. As an outcome of their work, within less than two years the company pared itself down into a much leaner operation and reaped benefits measured in billions of dollars. The company's efforts helped maintain dominant first or second market positions in two-thirds of the categories in which it competed worldwide.

This brings us back to the strategic process matrix introduced earlier in this chapter. Created by a senior executive team, it highlights cause-and-effect links between objectives and the vital few core processes. Once these are understood in the context of a whole enterprise's goals, performance gaps for each process are then calculated, allowing trade-offs between each process to become more evident (see Figure 5.5). Because each performance gap will be narrowed by making critical investments in human and financial resources, an executive team must prioritize them so that the whole is optimized. When gaps associated with each process are added, one gets a systemic snapshot of a company's competitive position.

The practical value of performance curves such as these was first perceived by Arthur Schneiderman during the mid-1980s when he served as vice-president for quality at Analog Devices. Based on re-

5.5. Using the strategic process matrix to calculate performance gaps.

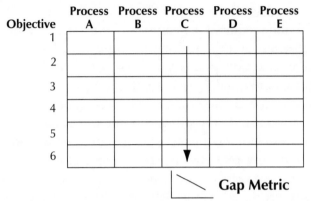

Strategic Performance Gaps
(at least one for each process)

search by his staff on numerous improvement curves applying to all sorts of processes, from mistakes made filling out forms, to defects in chip manufacturing, to error rates in product development, a revealing pattern emerged. Ten- to twenty-year improvement trend lines for all these activities showed a startlingly consistent similarity. Cut the measure of a weakness in half and it would take as long again to cut it in half, and yet again. If what he found was correct, it meant that one could predict the required level of competitive performance and the rate of improvement five to ten years forward.

❖ Ten- to twenty-year improvement trend lines for all these activities showed a startling consistent similarity. Cut the measure of a weakness in half and it would take as long again to cut it in half, and yet again.

Put into different words, he discovered that if a gap with a value of 100 existed between a capability on a given date and zero some time later, it would take the same amount of time to reduce the gap to 50 as it would to reduce the remaining 50 to 25, and the same amount of time to reduce the remaining 25 to 12.5, and so on.

Schneiderman coined this a "half-life improvement rate." From his staff's extensive studies he was able to establish rules of thumb for the half-life time required depending on two variables: the organizational complexity and the technical complexity of a process. A grid with nine intersection points was created on these two axes with half-life values indicated at each point (see Figure 5.6). The simplest processes at the lower left—such as a clerical input of data—had half-lives of one month. At the other extreme of complexity, at the top right, the most complex processes such as product development had half-lives of twenty-two months. This insight allowed him, and later the senior executive team at Analog Devices, to set improvement rates for key processes such as delivery with much more reasonable expectations of this being met. The company's worldwide plants, for example, were all required to achieve improvements in delivery capability at a steep improvement rate that was monitored quarterly. In this manner, a lackluster rate of delivery in the mid-1980s was brought to world–class levels within a few years.

5.6. Calculating half-life rates: Schneiderman's method.

[Measure = Months]

Organizational Complexity		Technical Complexity		
HI		14	18	22
MED		7	9	11
LO		1	3	5
		LO	MED	HI

Technical Complexity

Organizational complexity: based on number and variety of people or departments involved.
Technical complexity: based on the technical difficulty and variety of technologies being integrated.

For half-lives to be managed effectively, the performance curve must first measure a weakness, such as missed delivery time. The weakness would be the 15 percent late delivery time versus the strength, which is 85 percent on time. A theoretically achievable performance capability a number of years forward is calculated. At Analog Devices it was estimated to be no less than 1.5 percent late in five years. The gap is the difference between the two weakness points: 15 percent minus 1.5 percent, or 13.5 percent. By focusing on the weakness that must be narrowed, one can much more easily analyze and prioritize the root causes and attack them through breakthroughs or continuous improvement strategies (see Figure 5.7).

Out of such translations come tightly focused goals and realistic timetables for action teams to address. These, evidence shows, are far more motivating because cause and effect of day-to-day effort can be seen far more readily. Given the right curve and rate of improvement, a process team can brainstorm root causes using structured problem solving tools such as fishbone diagrams and Pareto charts, prioritize their importance, and thus make decisions on remedial actions. The proposed actions and the cumulative investments necessary to implement them across all key processes can be judged by a senior executive team.

If the results of this top-to-bottom analysis are widely communicated throughout an organization, the team responsible for a specific action will have a clear picture of the whole context within

5.7. Calculating half-life improvement rate: Schneiderman's method.

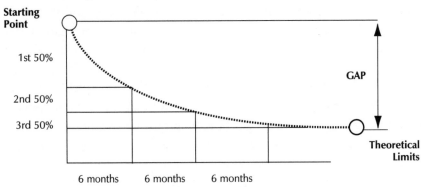

which a specific action will be taken. At Mitel, a maker of telephone switching systems in Wales, the sum total of this analysis is represented in a thorough and detailed planning matrix available for all to see. On it are depicted what needs to be done, how, by whom, and key measures of the expected outcomes. The company's managing director, Alan Kirkham, stated, "I'm a firm believer in visual management. Detailed information on our process walls tells everybody in the company—and our visitors—that we're absolutely open." (See Chapter 7 for the Mitel story.) Walls and doors that once established hierarchy and the obvious barriers to communication have been removed. "We've seen improvements of 300 percent in our business performance," said Kirkham, "and I have little doubt this is due in large part to having everyone seeing the whole."[8]

Why is this valuable? Simply by having access to a picture of the whole business, anyone in the organization can more easily adapt and change course without waiting for a directive from a boss. This ability is central to the success of the lean and flexible organization.

❖ By having access to a picture of the whole business, anyone in the organization can more easily adapt and change course without waiting for a directive from a boss.

The procedure of translating objectives into precisely targeted actions—systematized by one of the authors in the SPARK™ (Strategy and objectives, Performance gaps, Accountable teams, Rewards and recognition, and Knowledge management) methodology—is analogous to the policy deployment process instituted in many Japanese companies.[9] It starts with a directive from senior management that is deployed down into the three-tier system until there is overall consensus that all actions taken to ameliorate the directive will in fact optimize overall performance. In its strictest Japanese formulation, policy deployment is stiflingly bureaucratic and document-laden, a behavioral requirement vigorously resisted by Western managers. The latter, on the other hand, are far more open to delegating full responsibility to work teams, giving them latitude of judgment and less pressure to "dot the *i*'s" on required documentation. Hence the emphasis in the SPARK framework on assigning full accountability to teams and on designing rewards and recognition systems that acknowledge this shift in decision making.

Focusing on the vital few core processes is a three-tier technique that cascades downward. Senior management has its vital few strategic objectives and key processes, process-owning teams have their key performance gaps and half-life or breakthrough strategies, and action teams have their prioritized actions and implementation schedules. The pattern governing the system is based on Plan Do Check Act (PDCA) learning loops. Senior management works through an annual cycle that allows it to calibrate its strategic goals and to gauge the continued effectiveness of each process team's performance gap strategy. Each process team goes through its own annualized PDCA cycle to adjust its own pace of improvement and better guide the actions that carry out the Do phase. Appropriate new practices that emerge out of an ongoing PDCA learning cycle are then standardized and made part of the organization's tool kit of preferred methods and techniques.

The iterative learning cycle is a proven method, born in part out of the evolution of total quality management practices, that allows an organization to be proactive in response to change and far less reactive to crises. With established performance gaps and a well-calibrated rate of change, the pace can be managed through progressive learning cycles, each leading to a new performance capability. Sustaining such improvements requires continual attention and discipline, without which the effectiveness of a whole system will quickly deteriorate.

Part II, Doers, spotlights just such vulnerabilities and successes in companies working to implement the three-tier system.

NOTES

1. Writing about Analog Devices's experiences, Professor Robert Kaplan of Harvard Business School popularized the scorecard concept in the pages of the *Harvard Business Review.*
2. Remarks by Arthur Schneiderman are quoted from Chris Argyris and Donald

A. Schön, *Organizational Learning: A Theory of Action Perspective* (Reading, Mass.: Addison Wesley, 1978).

3. Arthur M. Schneiderman, "Metrics for the Order Fulfillment Process." Boxford, Mass., 1994.

4. John Fly, "Oh No! Management Systems." Presentation to the Center for Quality Management, Cambridge, Mass., 1994.

5. G. Dan Hutcheson and Jerry D. Hutcheson, "Technology and Economics in the Semiconductor Industry," *Scientific American* (January 1996), p. 54.

6. Schneiderman, "Metrics." Explaining the value of simple metrics, the author wrote: There is a potential danger of overcomplicating metrics to make them a "better" proxy for customer satisfaction. For example, one proposal for measuring the severity of late shipments to customers was a quadratic equation (using Taguchi's loss function) based on the number of days the order was late. The logic was that being two weeks late was more than twice as bad as being one week late, so the square of the number of weeks late should be used. Try explaining that definition to an associate with limited mathematical training."

7. Allen Ward, "The Second Toyota Paradox: How Delaying Decisions Can Make Better Cars Faster," *Sloan Management Review* (Spring 1995), p. 55.

8. Conversation with Dan Dimancescu.

9. SPARK™ was developed by the Technology and Strategy Group, Cambridge, Massachusetts.

PART II

Doers

Chapter 6

PREPARING FOR BATTLE

There are three ways to lose a battle,
the first is to be unaware of your opponent,
the second is to be unprepared for your opponent, and
the third is to show fear in the face of your opponent.

Book of Five Rings, an ancient guide to the practice
of the Samurai warrior

A little sign with the message quoted above hangs above the
director of operations' desk at a company we'll call Nature's
Best.★ The company owns a single manufacturing facility
producing yogurt and ice cream and sells its output to major food
retail chains. The message on the sign may be uncomplicated, but it
is the precept that inspires the management style and behavior of the
director, Joe Kovalik. It guides his actions as a strategist and leader
within his company.

As Kovalik likes to put it, "Business is a war. It is fought daily
between this company and the rate of change in our marketplaces.
My job is to ensure that the company is aware of change, prepared
for it, and capable of competing confidently in our current and fu-

★The name for the company, the operations director, and the company's products
are disguised.

79

ture markets. After twenty-five years with this company I wonder why this simple lesson has taken almost twenty years to learn."

❖ Business is a war. It is fought daily between this company and the rate of change in our marketplaces.

The day Kovalik rose in rank to become the operations director, he vowed that the company would change and the problems he had faced as a department manager would not be allowed to continue. However, his new office came with an inheritance: an in-tray of problems to be solved that remained from the previous occupant. It took only two days for him to become immersed in a minefield that continued to wall him further away from his vision. Far from being anything akin to a strategic leader of the business, Kovalik had little time to think coherently as more of his time was spent managing reactively than delegating and leading key processes for which he was held responsible. He jokingly suggested that, at the time, he was probably "the best-paid foreman in the yogurt business."

As Kovalik settled into his position, the business faced a major crisis. In the summer of 1986, the introduction of foreign brand-name ice cream and yogurts coupled with problems within the business caused a sharp decline in market share, and the company's reputation with industrial buyers of its product began to suffer. The effect of these events was to turn a previously profitable company into one in which every action was scrutinized by shareholders and customers. Despite the odds, the company struggled forward, patching holes and attempting to find a way out of the crisis and the threat that it would eventually collapse under the pressure.

IDENTIFYING THE PROBLEMS

To understand the problems faced by Nature's Best—problems faced by many companies—Kovalik and his fellow managers analyzed the symptoms and causes of the decline. It soon became clear that many of the difficulties resulted from problems rooted in the organization itself.

The first problem identified was a lack of internal channels of communication and direction. The development of a task-oriented system of functional specialization and narrowly focused departments had created an insularity and a preoccupation with accommodating change only within a single sphere of responsibility. Although every department manager had, with the best intentions, attempted to accommodate the needs of customers, individual performance metrics and the presence of many poorly aligned "islands of reform" had resulted in suboptimal performance. The misalignment of individual departmental strategies was exactly what Kovalik had inherited, and hence the manner in which he found himself having to work.

❖ The development of a task-focused system of functional specialization and narrowly focused departments had created an insularity and a preoccupation with accommodating change only within a single sphere of responsibility.

When Kovalik took office, the performance of the operations director was defined in three narrowly bounded measures: maximum machine utilization, maximum labor utilization, and low material costs. So Kovalik quite naturally ran his machines as hard as possible, with massive batches of production to maintain a low operations cost. Needless to say, this activity undermined the maintenance of the equipment, leading to breakdowns and frustrating the logistics department, which required a variety of finished stocks to ship to customers. Attempting maximum labor utilization also created problems; it was quite common for Kovalik to assign employees to non-production work, such as cleaning and other duties, to ensure that utilization remained high. The target of low material costs also proved elusive; as production batches grew, the company sucked in more and more raw material, wasted more, and significantly impaired the performance of the procurement department by demanding the expedition of materials and requiring higher and higher levels of material stocks.

The fragmentation of responsibilities created by functional specialization and the lack of interest in activities in other departments emerged as a fundamental cause of many of the problems faced by the company. Clearly, the enterprise's activities needed to be aligned so that any aspect of the operation could be understood by all the other areas. And just as important was cultivating an understanding that the customer service offered by Nature's Best could aspire to flawlessness only when all functions worked together in a coordinated manner.

❖ Nature's Best could aspire to flawlessness only when all functions worked together in a coordinated manner.

Another realization came when the management team began to analyze the external environment and the rate of change demanded of the business. When the company was established in 1954, ice cream was a popular consumer product. Industrial buyers bought simply to keep the store shelves well stocked. However, as time progressed new consumer expectations affected every activity of the business. Better delivery and quality performance were demanded of the company by increasingly sophisticated industrial buyers and by a need to meet more stringent customer preferences for taste and variety. The level of change experienced by Nature's Best and each internal department mirrored what companies in other industries, from cars to retailing to consumer electronics, experienced worldwide. The steep performance improvement curves experienced over a four-decade period by this one company (see Figure 6.1), making day-to-day management increasingly more complex, are a lesson in the relentlessness of change.

During the development of the company from the late 1950s to the 1990s, all major process performance measures were subject to frequent change, each resulting in a new and more detailed measure. But under the traditional departmental system, these changes were accommodated by a task-oriented departmental structure. As a consequence, problems induced by changes in the external environment were exaggerated by internal lack of alignment.

A simple qualitative performance measure is the amount of

6.1. Nature's best "customer-facing" rate of change (1954–1996): Where will they have to be in 2000 or 2010?

Performance Measure	1950s	1970s	1990s	Department Responsible for Change Management
Quality	Not measured	Called "shrinkage"	Percentages Parts per million	Quality control
Delivery	Once a month	Once a week	Twice a week	Logistics & traffic
Costing	Cost plus margin	Cost plus acceptable margin	Market determined (target costs)	Accounts
Rate of new product introduction	One or two a year	Three or four a year	Six to ten a year	Product design
Product life cycle	Decades	Six years	One to two years	Sales & marketing
Inventory turns	Ten to twelve	Fifteen to twenty	Fifty plus	Manufacturing & operations

product that the company wastes in producing a product for sale. In the 1950s, industrial buyers and most competitors in the ice cream business simply assumed that waste was inevitable in the manufacture and supply of ice cream. But by the 1970s, the company had begun to track the waste of materials by percentage, and industrial buyers had begun to demand that service quality be measured as well. Twenty years later the measure had changed again to embrace the concept of parts per million of defect levels of products and service quality. To put this into perspective, a single percentage point of rejects is the same as ten thousand parts per million defects. In 1974, to cope with this level of imperfection, the company created another department. As might be expected given the problem it was formed to manage, it was named Quality Control. The new department was given total responsibility to counteract these pressures and external demands. This process worked reasonably well, and despite a long learning curve, the department managed to contain the problems and prevent any serious crises from occurring.

In the company's attempt to raise performance quality, however, the quality control department quite obviously was only one link in a chain of departments that influence the management of quality. Given this departmental structure, the favored management approach to tackling a cross-company problem was to issue directives to other areas of the business. But even top-down control did not guarantee successful resolution of a problem. This was particularly so when the directive interfered with and seemingly limited the performance of another department. Poor internal alignment around common problems, it eventually became evident, was compounded by a poor response to managing the change process at a company-wide level. This meant that although changes designed to improve a single measure of departmental effectiveness were comparatively easy to accomplish, the real problem affecting the rate of change across the whole company simultaneously was next to impossible. The aggregation of fragmented changes was leading to an inevitable decline of Nature's Best.

❖ Although changes designed to improve a single measure of departmental effectiveness were comparatively easy to accomplish, the real problem of affecting the rate of change across the whole company simultaneously was next to impossible.

"In short," commented Kovalik, "we had no mechanism to control and direct change on a companywide scale. It simply did not exist, and therefore not only had we failed to be aware of change demanded of the company, we were not prepared for it either, and consequently we showed fear when we attempted change in the face of our customers. It was not a pleasant learning experience."

THE AWAKENING

Having come to terms with the company's systemic weaknesses, management fought on through the busy summer demand period of 1986, the year in which Nature's Best first faced stiff competition from foreign brands. Toward the low season in the business calendar, when the day-to-day firefights subsided, managers were ready to tackle more proactive activities. Fall was generally the preferred time for the ritual annual business planning meeting to review past performance and create the short- and medium-term strategies for the coming year and beyond. The meeting typically consisted of a managerial tug-of-war for resources and finger pointing by each department to blame other functional areas for lower performance figures.

This particular year, however, there were *no* resources and plenty of opinions why the company had declined. Few, however, were based on factual information. Thus, after a period of the ritual blame game, the managers still faced the inevitable question, Will the company survive another year? During the annual planning meeting, a dramatic step was taken. It was agreed that the current situation presented such a threat that the managers had no option but to investigate the causes of the problems and take steps to address the fundamental failings of the business in its entirety. It was understood, too, that the process of change would take a period of years. The creation of a stable environment of cooperation and collaboration would be designed to increase visibility and interaction among departments. The management team also decided that an infrastructure needed to be built at many levels in the organization to more fully coordinate and integrate the activities of each area. The management team would thus have full control over the direction of the business and lower-level cross-functional teams would take responsibility for enacting change within the company. Creating a shared information network would free key business processes from the domination of any single department. Companywide enactment groups, guided by process "champions," could therefore avoid the frustration and uncertainty otherwise associated with trying to change an entire operating system one department at a time. This course of action was agreed to, and, although immediate measures were needed to ameliorate the current situation, the management team took full responsibility for identifying internal needs and for integrating customers into the process of managing the business.

NEW CONFIDENCE

Despite a period of layoffs in 1989, several years later Nature's Best produces higher volumes of business at a fraction of the cost in 1986. The company is also actively involved with its customers in predicting and determining future rates of change in the industry and plans to open a second factory in the near future. The directors, including Kovalik, of what is now acknowledged to be a truly lean enterprise have undergone a radical transformation. They now direct the business from desks free of mounds of paperwork. They are doing what they are supposed to do and finding that they enjoy it too. That is why the sign that hangs on the wall in Kovalik's office is a sign of the times. A decade earlier, it could easily have been replaced by a sign that read simply Closed hanging from the factory gates.

The lessons learned by Nature's Best are not unique. They have been repeated time and again in the best companies in the world over, proving that no company in today's global economy can live in the comfort of having a "safe product" or a "safe market." Neither can a company, regardless of its past performance, believe itself to have a "right" to continued survival. Just ask the likes of Howard Johnson's restaurants or Fokker airplanes. Or ask those that have battled back, like British Steel or Chrysler, whom so many had written off as candidates for terminal bankruptcy.

The fundamental lesson from Nature's Best is that organizational design can be proactively managed. The cross–organizational transparency needed to support the lean enterprise can be achieved by identifying key processes that operate within and beyond the walls of the business. The 1986 crisis at Nature's Best created the focus needed for a reactive management team, separated by departmental boundaries, to act as a single cohesive unit in planning and executing the future development of the business.

Chapter 7

MANAGING
WITHOUT TITLES

I'm a believer in the big bang.

Alan Kirkham,
Managing Director of Mitel Telecom

The first thing you notice about Alan Kirkham, the managing director of Mitel Telecom, is how relaxed he seems. "We have no titles here and most importantly," he recently said emphatically, "nobody owns anything. I tell everyone that there is no job for life at Mitel. For myself I'm just the head coach." By this he means no one "owns" budgets, employees, or facilities. Even the word *employee* is being phased out in favor of the designation *associates*. Looking ahead to a different kind of relationship, Kirkham added, "There'll be a time when associates may want to be self-employed and hire themselves back to the company." Statements such as this are enough to make a manager of the "old school" shudder.

Introduced in Chapter 5 as a man who eliminates walls—including those around his own office—Kirkham has worked with his own internal team to craft a wholly new type of enterprise in which process is clearly the strategy and old ways are definitely out. Kirkham recounts a moment of revelation triggered in 1988 when he walked through the front door of his company's modern Welsh facility with a large sign around his neck reading Order. He asked the bewildered receptionist to treat him as a customer "order" to be channeled through the system. "I did this," he said, "because I noted something very paradoxical in the sales staff. Salesmen would return ecstatic with a customer order in hand, but, within hours, doom would descend on them as they confronted the chore of pushing the order over endless hurdles."

Kirkham's attention-getting "order" experiment revealed to the whole company two unforgettable things: (1) the process was broken into disconnected bits, some of which were dead ends where people actually said, "I don't know what to do next," and (2) no one "owned" the whole process. It was evident to him that Mitel would not survive if it did not change its hierarchical management style dominated by functions that owned resources but in which no one owned critical processes that served customers. This incident was just one step in a ten-year journey that started for Kirkham in the mid-1980s and culminated in 1996 with the formal institution of a process-driven strategy in which titles and ownership of resources are things of the past.

❖ The process was broken into disconnected bits, some of which were dead ends where people actually said, "I don't know what to do next."

MITEL'S BACKGROUND

Mitel is located in the heart of Wales's famed coal-mining (now vanished) and steel production country. Within sight of the company's modern, glass-sheathed buildings is a sprawling British Steel plant on the borders of the Severn River, itself witness to thousands of years of history, including the eventful years of the most famed of British kings, Arthur, who reigned from southeastern Wales fifteen hundred years earlier. Wales, its coal mines closed, graded, and carefully grassed over, is now home to dozens of foreign transplants, including forty-five from Japan—the likes of Matsushita, Sony, and

Toyota—and, more recently, arrivals from Taiwan and Korea attracted by public subsidies and labor rates that are reputed to be lower than Korean working wages.

A subsidiary of its parent company headquartered in Ontario, Canada, Mitel-U.K. holds almost 14 percent of the national market for state-of-the-art business communication systems. Its clients buy hardware and software products that provide communication "lines" in quantities as few as a handful to as many as ten thousand. But unlike its giant competitors—British Telecom, Northern Telecom, and AT&T—Mitel offers "open systems" capabilities. According to Fred Hadwick, responsible for the channel management and support process, "this means that one can plug anyone else's equipment into our system. The client is not stuck with our system and none else." To make this happen Mitel has created families of semiconductors that make this open interfacing possible. The chips are so good and so useful that most of its big-name competitors buy the chips for themselves. "We've always been recognized as a technology leader," said Hadwick. "What's really different now from just a few years ago is that we've become much more of a systems integrator starting in 1994. We offer full solutions to a customer and not just a box with some features."

From a day-to-day point of view, this has made life much more complicated. Products are now tailored to single users, work groups, whole enterprises, and even to multicompany networks. The implications are not trivial if one begins to consider that such an approach allows individuals and groups to make buying decisions that would otherwise have been made by a centralized information department. Even the company's colorful new foldout visiting cards are a sign of the times. Under Hadwick's name, instead of an organizational title, is Convergence Activist. To the immediate "What's that?" the backside offers the following:

> *convergence.* Facilitating enriched, effective communications between people regardless of *distance, time, media,* or *language.*

Behind this language is a corporate ambition to be the leader in marrying voice communication, normally done by telephone networks, to data communication, normally done through electronic networks called LANs or WANs. "This will allow us to put multi-media on the desktop," said Mick Leonard, whose business card also reads Convergence Activist. "This has an organizational implication at our client companies," he added, "especially when one considers that the 'telephone' is administered by one group and 'data' by another." All of this has a direct bearing on how Mitel has chosen to change the way it does business. "Ten years ago," recalled Hadwick, "the span of technology you needed to master was much narrower. Now in one day you may have to be able to field customer calls on voice mail, data networks, LANs, or videoconferencing." But there is also an equally fundamental change that has occurred: "Not that long ago, the majority of my intellectual energy went into organizational battles. You fought to protect your corner. Now, we channel a majority of our energy into the business issues through process teams that deliver real value to our customers."

THE TURNING POINT

The evolution has brought Mitel to a critical turning point. It has fully embraced doing business through five key processes: product and market direction (which deals with larger strategic questions), product development, demand creation, change management and support, and order fulfillment. Employees engaged in the last three processes interface directly with persons in the company's channels, the distributors of its products and services. For each process there is a "champion," whose responsibility it is to ensure that the process is understood, supported, and implemented successfully by action teams. An operations team, which sits together in a wallless open area, oversees the interaction of these five key processes and deliberates the allocation of investment out of operating income as well as product and market direction. Driving performance is a set of seven measures championed by another member of the senior team, Ken Bailey: operating income, gross margins, channel satisfaction, employee satisfaction, new product sales, return on investment, and value added per employee. (The word *associate* has not yet crept into the language of the measurement system.)

The basic components of every process and those involved in executing it are mapped out on walls within a large comfortable war room with swivel chairs and a coffee machine offering ten choices of brews. The company performance measures are also plotted, with improvements or downturns openly charted. These measurements, of course, are open for anyone in the company to scrutinize and discuss; and, as underscored in Chapter 5, this is a primary reason in Alan Kirkham's view that business results have jumped 300 percent in three years. "Being able to see the whole has inspired an entirely new level of capability and energy," he observed.

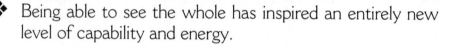 Being able to see the whole has inspired an entirely new level of capability and energy.

THE JOURNEY

Kirkham and Mitel still have a long journey ahead, and he knows the path will be neither easy nor straight. He joined Mitel in 1984. "This was a time when the firm operated hierarchically, which really meant that it operated with reflexes that were risk averse," he recalled. "Change was not seen in a good light. In a fragmented hierarchical structure all you needed was for one person to say no and nothing would happen. There were at least seven management layers then."

Recalling his youth as a rugby player, Kirkham drew on that experience for an intuitive awareness that there was clearly a better way to go about organizing. "When I was about nineteen or twenty, I was on a team which really didn't have a single great player. But we were regarded as one of the strongest U.K. teams then." The lesson stuck with him: One can do more than ever expected by functioning as a team even if the individuals are not always superstars. Many years later, in the mid-1980s, these instincts would draw him quickly to the inherent strengths of the total quality management (TQM) movement. "I became one of three trainers at the company and trained at least 500 people, he said. What struck me then as fundamental was that everything about TQM treated work as processes—yet here we were bureaucratized into management layers."

But zeal overtook the company. "We just went too far." Every process was mapped: 800 of them. Procedures were documented: 4,000 of them. "We did this in great part to satisfy ISO 9000 requirements," he stated. "But when you got right down to it all that documentation added absolutely nothing to the value of our business." He recalled awards being given out to TQM teams—there were at least sixty of them—for doing all this analysis and documentation. It took a while to realize that those awards were not rewarding actual value-adding work but only the following of procedures.

❖ We just went too far. Every process was mapped: 800 of them. Procedures were documented: 4,000 of them.

For a period of several years, from 1989 to 1992, the company found itself stuck on a plateau. Things just were not improving. "We were well aware that we had enormously complex processes," said Kirkham, "and that we were allowing individual changes in them to happen here and there. But each of these changes had rippling effects that set everything else out of whack." In short, there was no systemic approach to managing the company's affairs, and TQM had not brought any radical insight into how to escape the trap of over-documented rituals. "I did know, however," acknowledged Kirkham, "that the principles underlying TQM were themselves sound: 'Do what you say'; 'Work toward zero defects'; 'Model your processes.' "

About this time the business process reengineering wave was beginning to take hold, and it caught Kirkham's attention. "What intrigued me most," he recalled, "was the optimistic talk about achieving rapid and significant cost savings and doubling customer satisfaction. We just got hooked." Looking back several years later, he quickly added that those dreams were never fulfilled. This insight coincided with several other factors all pointing to the need for radical change. A 51 percent ownership in Mitel by British Telecom was divested and bought by private investors. The same year, Kirkham, who already carried the title of vice-president, was made managing director of U.K. operations, including responsibility for sales in Europe, Africa, and the Middle East.

Kirkham chose this point, also coinciding with a recessionary slowdown in sales, to hand pick six senior managers whom he considered open-minded, good thinkers, and representative of all areas of the company. Freeing them of line responsibilities, he gave these high-profile managers one year to start with a clean slate and figure out how to better manage the "customer facing" front end of the business. Appropriately the effort was called "Project Front End." After nine months of extensive study, around Christmas of 1993, the managers came back with a plan. Out of this came a new operating model. The company would be flattened by eliminating unnecessary layers of management. Even the traditional concept of "managers" was to be thrown out, and people would be redeployed around processes. "What we wanted was to throw out the notion of managers directing the work of other people," said Kirkham. "We wanted them to think of designing processes that met customer expectations."

❖ The company would be flattened by eliminating unnecessary layers of management. Even the traditional concept of "managers" was to be thrown out, and people would be redeployed around processes.

All of this—for better or worse—was implemented. The worse did not take long to strike. The Project Front End team, some of the company's best people, returned to normal duties only to find their original responsibilities taken over by others. And their new assignments degraded their professional esteem. Five of the six quit the company in anger and frustration. "This was something we had not done the slightest to anticipate," said Kirkham, "and we failed terribly in not accounting for their well-being. We just charged ahead and in the process generated a lot of resentment." By his own acknowledgment there had been no effort to understand profound behavior changes implied in a move to a process-oriented style of management. "Those nice BPR [Business Process Re-engineering] headlines about all the dramatic benefits just didn't happen." And in a no-questions-asked step, Kirkham stopped the whole thing in its tracks.

❖ Those nice BPR headlines about all the dramatic benefits just didn't happen.

Fortunately, another project had been originated in 1993 along with Project Front End. Under the acronym SPRINT (Swift PRoduct INTroduction), effort was put into building an internal coalition favoring a team approach to managing product development. This was a time when the entire telecommunications industry was being awoken from its monopolistic slumber and having to act far more nimbly in response to customer needs. By 1994, the concepts had been sufficiently studied to warrant implementation; and in a bold style characteristic of Kirkham, SPRINT teams became the way to do business. People left work on a Friday. The next Monday they were expected to work on teams. This not only generated enormous confusion of roles but an immediate tug-of-war for the best "star" performers to work on too many teams. Helping to sort out this confusion was Fred Hadwick, who created a compelling story to share companywide about the SPRINT process. This allowed eight or nine project teams to be formed and co-located in their own spaces, thereby challenging the functional system, in which individual members were "owned" as part of departmental head counts.

Two years later, after trial and error and considerable searching for the best practices and useful insights wherever they could be found, Mitel started to see its way. The pattern that is now falling into place was drawn by Kirkham in the form of a simple inverted pyramid. "There are five key roles that one fits into at Mitel-U.K. today." At the bottom are two operations teams with five members each. The task of each is to identify new opportunities for half their time and to keep the pulse of day-to-day operations the other half.

Next on the inverted pyramid are two self-explanatory enclosures, one entitled "Team Leader" and the other "Support Specialists." Next up is a wide horizontal box labeled "Teams." Above it, at the top, is a larger box labeled "Customers." In short, one's identity at Mitel comes from playing within anyone of those boxes. One's career and reward path is paced by one's skills and competence improvement.

It is in this setting that old-style hierarchical titles have vanished. "We all have internal roles," said Kirkham. These have names like "coach," "champion" (of a process), "team leader," "skills champion," and "team member." The role of coach is not what is commonly meant when other companies use the term. At Mitel, each associate takes the initiative to identify one or several individuals to coach him or her in a selected area. Much like a mentoring process, this allows internal skills and knowledge to be distributed to those who need and want them most. "In my own case," said Kirkham, "I have seven people coaching me from all types of activities within the company." But the real world still requires that titles be used—when dealing with customers, for example. They still want to know who the managing director is, who the sales rep is, or who the representative from engineering is. So associates are allowed to print those titles on cards as needed.

What are the results after three years of this most recent evolutionary step? At the end of the second year the company achieved a profit target of 300 percent and remained on track for doubling its sales during the third year. This made Mitel-U.K. a star performer and a candidate for public attention, including national television features and increasing flows of visitors to see how the new management system worked. But more sobering to Kirkham is the surprising realization that in this period "we have done nothing to improve our customer satisfaction [it has stayed flat], and most alarmingly our employee satisfaction has declined severely." It is evident from this reading that something is working but that a serious human component of the equation was given short shrift. Not surprisingly, number one on Kirkham's list of priorities is to champion people issues.

Is there a model in all this? "I don't know," answered Kirkham.

"We definitely want to be a model of information management. After all, if we don't preach what we practice, why should anyone want to buy solutions from us?" Reflecting on how the outside world is evolving, he clearly believes that at least a third of the larger U.K. companies "just don't understand what we are talking about and will get wiped out." Another third, he believes, know that this is all about the future but don't really have a blueprint. And of the final third who are really doing it, he said, "What I see emerging from a lot of BPR is a new version of the old matrix management with a functional boss on one side and a project boss on another. That's not what true process management is all about."

Chapter 8

REAPING THE BENEFITS

Because lateral processes decentralize general management decisions, they free up top management for other decisions. Thus they increase the capacity of the organization to make more decisions more often. The organization is therefore more adaptable to constant change.

Jay R. Galbraith, *Designing Organizations* (Reading, Mass.: Addison Wesley, 1995)

The importance of ready adaptability to change is illustrated by transitions occurring in the retail industry of countries like Great Britain, one of the most dynamic marketplaces in the world. In 1992 the industry consisted of some twenty-eight thousand outlets, a drop of more than 40 percent from 1984 in the wake of strong domestic competition, acquisitions by the major retailers, and supply chain streamlining. The remaining leading supermarkets have emerged as models of world-class performance when it comes to delivery of value to more and more demanding customers. Although the British market is large and diverse, it is dominated by eight major supermarket chains, each owning many hundreds of stores. (The top three retailers account for more than fifteen hundred stores in the United Kingdom alone.) Accounting for less than 10 percent of the total outlets in the market but over 70 percent of the total industry sales volume, the "Big Eight" are reshaping future trading and supply chain management strategies as competitive foundations for entering new international markets. By tackling key delivery processes systemically, this elite group is determining the shape of the performance improvement curve, forcing the remaining British outlets to lag substantially behind. How this evolution occurred in a process-driven strategy can be seen through the experience of the market leader, Tesco Stores Limited, the barometer of Britain's retailing vitality.

BRITISH FOOD RETAILING: TESCO

With particularly elegant, peak-roofed buildings that have altered the architectural appeal of the retailing landscape, Tesco, the industry trendsetter, is a focal point for some 2,000 vendors that support almost 525 company-owned stores. The driving force within the Tesco system is an aggressive quality, cost, and delivery program intended to create an experience that "delights" customers.

THE NORTH AMERICAN GOLIATH: WAL-MART

It is truly a merchandising giant. Sales in 1995 totaling $93 billion and 675,000 employees make the firm bigger than IBM or General Electric. When a customer walks through the checkout counter, the information captured at the register flows directly to the supplier's plant. The data is forwarded and includes all the necessary scheduling information on shipment dates, amounts, locations, and the best method of shipping. Reputedly the owner of the largest installed computer system (outside of the U.S. Department of Defense), Wal-Mart has used its vast electronic network as a competitive weapon. By helping to eliminate vendor sales representatives and distributors, this one step—difficult as it was to engineer—took almost 30 percent of the cost out of retail prices.

Wal-Mart imposed new ways of doing business on its suppliers, including giant ones such as Procter & Gamble (P&G) (one-third Wal-Mart's size), which calculates that 11 percent of its sales are booked by this one client. This means shipping an estimated 100 million or more cases of goods a year. The two companies use an intercompany team to manage their buyer/seller relationship, working as a group in their own combined site. More than seventy P&G employees participate. The shared sense of purpose coupled with hard-driving profit and volume objectives helped triple sales for P&G from $500 in 1989 to $1.5 billion by the end of 1992.

For Tesco in the late 1970s, things were quite different. It was managed as a paper-intensive and thus predominantly manual bureaucratic ordering system that guessed at customer demand and relayed delivery information to vendors by mail. Operations were centered around individual store managers who acted in isolation from all other store managers. To link demand with supply, vendor representatives would visit a store at regular intervals to collect orders and transfer them back to the home office. In time, however, consumer expectations began to change and competitive pressure mounted. This eventually caused a series of worsening stresses and strains in the whole food-retailing system.

During this earlier period, a customer walking into a Tesco store would select his or her needs from a choice of 10,000 individual products. To meet demand, some of the higher-traffic stores received up to fifty truck deliveries each day, dispatched from twenty-two regional warehouses owned by the company. An annual tally of shipment added up to about 50 million cases of product across the entire chain of stores. The system's growing complexity and fragility was evident in the company's use of average levels of product availability as a performance measure. These rarely surpassed 92 percent, meaning that being out of stock was an accepted way of doing business. Eventually customers started complaining and competitors began to fill the gap. By 1980, the inefficiencies of this supply system were so great that the company saw declines both in market share and its image with customers.

To tackle the problem, senior executives made a measured but radical—and risky—decision. They would centralize all decision making at a single corporate office. This would be done at the very same time that other major players were in the thick of doing just the opposite, decentralizing control to the store level.

❖ To tackle the problem, senior executives made a measured but radical—and risky—decision. They would centralize all decisionmaking at a single corporate office.

By centralizing management and information flows, Tesco aimed to orchestrate its extended vendor supply chain with an aggressive business plan. The latter called for substantial cost decreases in managing the tentacular supply system, guaranteeing lead times, eliminating delays and duplication of effort, and integrating suppliers within a newly created central distribution hub. To support all this, the company instituted a comprehensive training program tied to three new *processes,* each critical to the business. One focused on stock management, another on commercial trading, and a third on distribution.

Vendor contact with Tesco was redirected to a single centralized "owner" for each process. New information technology and systems were also introduced to facilitate more appropriate and time-sensitive management decisions. This information platform was shared with vendors by integrating them into an Electronic Data Interchange (EDI) system allowing electronic trading. In addition, to attain quality, cost, and delivery goals, the company made advances in the physical logistics system by reducing the number of warehouses from twenty-two to eight multipurpose units. These facilities were designed to handle all forms of goods, including frozen products and perishables with short shelf lives. Each had dedicated delivery vehicles with chambers for handling frozen and nonperishable goods simultaneously.

The convergence of the three processes—stock management, commercial trading, and distribution—also attacked a problem endemic to the food-retailing industry: demand amplification. This meant that minor movements in stock at the store level mushroomed into larger movements at the warehouses and even greater demand on suppliers. To reduce unnecessary supply chain hyperactivity, Tesco management decided that stores should receive only two shipments a day. The cutback actually increased delivery and store-level service performance of the company. It also decreased operational costs and increased the quality of information from vendors and their presentation of products to the stores. This proved an effective solution to what had been a highly fragmented operation easily capable of going out of control. Simplicity of execution was the key success factor. In this case, less meant more.

❖ Simplicity of execution was the key success factor. In this case, less meant more.

Equally important was a commitment, novel in the industry, to creating a partnership process with suppliers and a team to manage it. At its inception, ten vendors were selected to be integrated into the centralized information system operated by Tesco. These suppliers received and transmitted information covering all aspects of the order process, including selection of the thirty-minute delivery slot when they were ready to ship stock to a Tesco warehouse. The new coordinated alignment of processes diminished the need to overestimate product stocks for the network of stores. This in turn diminished the impact of demand amplification on the supply base. Through such measures, the company made its operations increasingly transparent and extended the benefits of an integrated three-tier teaming approach to its supplier community. The success of the partnership-process team encouraged Tesco to integrate even more suppliers. Four hundred vendors had joined the system by 1983; ten years later the information web extended to approximately 2,000 integrated suppliers operating not just in the United Kingdom but worldwide.

❖ One-time entry and open access to data by all on-line suppliers allows each one to probe the dynamics of the supply chain and thus better manage his own stock levels.

Illustrating the impact of the new management system, Tesco now handles 96 percent of all purchases centrally, maintains half the corporate levels of stock that it once did, and delivers three times more produce variety to its customers, or about 26,000 items per store. To enhance the system further, the company uses point-of-sale data capture and has fully integrated warehouses by introducing mobile computers. One-time entry and open access to data by all on-line suppliers allows the suppliers to probe the dynamics of the supply chain and thus better manage their own stock levels.

TESCO: A DECADE OF CHANGE	1982–1983	1992–1993
Stock turns	13	32
Service levels (to store)	92%	98.5%
Sales	$3.0 billion	$11.4 billion
Stock coverage (inventory)	21 days	12.79 days
Warehouses	Decentralized	Centralized
Order Processing	Manual/Fax	EDI
Order placement to goods received time	128 hours	24 hours
Central Distribution (cases)	50 million	475 million

As one might say, these are numbers to write home about. In fact, they meant that by the early 1990s Tesco had surpassed its original business plan. Industry analysts give the company a favorable competitive rating in almost all critical categories. Demonstrating its competitive achievements in delivery, quality, and cost, Tesco operates with only two thirds of the inventory needed by its closest rivals, and the company manages the time from confirming an order to the receipt of the product to as little as 24 hours, down from 120 hours.

COMPARING BRITISH FOOD RETAILERS:
The Number of Days Stock (Inventory) Coverage, 1994

Tesco	12.79
Competitor 1	18.83
Competitor 2	25.79
Competitor 3	25.90
Competitor 4	35.55

Tesco has grown to 110,000 employees serving the needs of about 10 million customers who visit its distinctive stores each week. The company continues to innovate and reinvent itself and thus reshape the industry performance curves. Recognizing the new importance of its key strategic processes and desiring to integrate the external capabilities of vendors in this improvement process, Tesco's executive team has also created the new position of supply chain director.

To complete the circle of improvements and interweave the

activities undertaken by the many process teams, Tesco conducts a system of annual policy reviews. This allows the executive team to assess the direction and velocity of companywide improvement activities and to check the alignment of the enterprise with the market environment and with industry performance. These assessments result in new operating plans and reprioritizing of activities, thereby translating objectives into actions to be carried out by teams at lower levels in the organization. The strategies of the company have become more and more demanding and challenging, but what is absolutely certain is that there is no turning back.

Chapter 9

THE FRONT LINE

If each function optimizes its costs, it is invariably to the detriment of the total cost of a project. In contrast, if one brings all functions together around a project, the solution is far more likely to be optimized.

Yves Dubreil, creator of the Renault Twingo, in *Industries et Techniques,* July 1996.

After decades of functional silos and task-based DAISY [Do As I Say, You!] management, it is hardly surprising that almost every business in the world seems to have a poster, located in a corridor or coffee area, extolling employees to WORK SMARTER NOT HARDER. Rarer are the clues as to how this is done.

Imagine a customer call in the "good old days" of hard work. The customer would speak to a polite receptionist and be transferred to a person with a partial answer, then to another, and probably to a few more before the frustrated customer managed to piece together the whole answer. Imagine, alternatively, a single office space and a co-located "smart" team at work managing the operations of the business. Each member is equipped with a computer that provides shared access to current files on the customer, the customer's order, and other pertinent data. A customer can call any one team member and get a complete answer. Under such circumstances, an immediate decision can be provided without delay and without transferring phone calls.

As the third tier of the three-tier system, the action team is both a part and an extension of the traditional role of the manager. Rather than formally specifying the expected behavior of individuals, the process "owner" delegates authority to act within well-specified goals and constraints. This frees time for the manager to contemplate the future direction of improvement efforts while the team targets and implements improvements that will narrow critical performance gaps. With members drawn from operational competencies and skills within the business, action teams are small and highly focused. As in the foregoing example, they are commonly co-located. Often they are part of an aggregation of small teams grouped in a common area. At Chrysler's vast Tech Center, a new-car team consists of 750 engineers on a single open floor arranged in small-team clusters. Under the new rules, the manager does not participate in the daily operations of the team but provides directional leadership and support and acts as the final arbiter when needed to resolve unexpected problems. This role is also treated more and more as that of a coach. For Peter Bachman, a Borg Warner site operations director, the change to empowering teams has affected his own well-being. "My teams allow me to sleep peacefully at night," he will tell anyone enthusiastically.

Reinterpretations of the status of the team leader are implied, too. "I sat down one day with one of the teams during our 'lunch box' sessions," recalled Bryan Jackson, director of Toyota Motor Company of the United Kingdom. "Team members can ask questions of their team leaders. One question had to do with our cost system, and someone asked me to speak and I answered him directly. His response was quite simply that my answer was great and that I should keep up the good work."

Dave Meisner at American Standard's Plumbing Division had long known that day-to-day work could be better accomplished by teams—and not by simply delegating tasks. This was high in his mind when he was transferred from the United States to a company site in Mittlich, Germany. As a newly appointed product development process owner, he was free to redesign the way in which work got accomplished. "No easy task," he recalled, "given that new ideas run headlong into thick walls, particularly in Germany." His engineering group consisted of forty-eight people. Not surprisingly, the product development operation, small as it was, was organized and built to support functional groups. Making matters worse was a traditional office layout in which corridors with closed doors demarcated specialized work areas. In one space five mechanical engineers sat together. In another sat two electronics specialists; and in yet another, six computer-aided design (CAD) specialists. Packaging, testing, the sample shop, and technical, graphics, and writing were all in separate groupings and spaces. Product development was coordinated by small groups that called on these skills as needed.

Meisner wrestled with a strict corporate mandate for process owners to create a work-team environment, but he also realized that things as basic as the building's architecture were solidly in the way. His solution, implemented within the following twelve months, was simple and elegant. Four teams, each one focused on the development of a single type of product, replaced the old functional organization chart. There were no other boxes on the chart. Each action team had a leader, core members and additional members bringing specialized competencies to bear. The largest group had thirteen members; the smallest, seven. This led also to a reduction in manpower need by eight people.

To accommodate the new system, Meisner realized that he would have to physically gut the building they were located in and radically alter the layout. What ensued was a space designed to accommodate the four product development teams. Each team aligned seating and desks along the walls or with table surfaces extending into the shared space. High-powered workstations loaded with the latest CAD systems and software allowed every team to have real-time access to the others' work and to a common database. Almost sacrilegiously, doors were eliminated between each team space. The open layout forced people to walk through other teams' space, thereby providing opportunities for casual "nonlinear" interactions and discussions. From an operational point of view, these co-located action teams could now focus on a specific project and, in fact, take full responsibility as a group for its completion. In addition, four individuals served as a support group to each team: Meisner as the process owner for product development; a process owner for predevelopment; a coach/trainer for the CAD systems; and an enabler/consultant to reinforce building codes and standards awareness.

❖ To accommodate the new system, Meisner realized that he would have to physically gut the building they were located in and radically alter the layout.

Action teams such as those designed by Meisner are small and highly motivated channels for the execution of process performance objectives. With imagination and effort, these teams become a natural structure allowing the free flow of information between individuals sharing a common task. Indeed, people that witness such teams in action are often surprised at the noise levels they hear. At Calsonic Llanelli Radiators new technology center in Wales, there is constant chatter between small groups who work at tables allowing four individuals to face one another in a larger open space. Teams in such environments can be likened to the trading rooms of a stock exchange, where a constant, audible flow of information is vital to making rapid decisions.

❖ Teams in such environments can be likened to the trading rooms of a stock exchange, where a constant, audible flow of information is vital to making rapid decisions.

By responding quickly to uncertainty and by making decisions having immediate effect on customer service, these teams become extensions of the customer and in many cases integrate with the customer to such an extent that the distinction between the company and customer becomes increasingly blurred. Location of teams is another critical variable. An example of an action team having such an impact on customer service is demonstrated by the Lane Group, a leading British logistics and services company founded in 1964 to support manufacturers and retailers. At The Body Shop, Lane delivery team members intermeshed with the customer to such an extent that the team located itself at the headquarters of The Body Shop, 150 miles away from the headquarters of the Lane Group. Such a seamless service approach makes it almost impossible to see the boundary between the customer and the Lane Group.

At Lane's meetings concerning the working of the overall "delivery process," action teams participate to ensure that all the customer requirements are being met and to provide immediate performance feedback on the status of the company. CEO Rebecca Jenkins makes it a personal priority to meet with customers at least every six months to review performance and discuss the future direction of the businesses. This is combined with an "open book" system between the companies allowing all costs to be reviewed in order to find new ways of contributing to the success of the customer.

❖ All our employees are extensions of the partners' work force, so they know and respect the products.

This level of customer service has enabled Lane and its customers to develop new capabilities. "Our success is based on a partnership approach," commented Jenkins, along with "quality of service, and a commitment to meet the ever changing needs of our clients. For instance, we are keen to portray the customers' products in the best way possible to the end consumer, so we have developed new technologies and operating practices. All our employees are extensions of the partners' work force, so they know and respect the products."[1]

POINT—AND GET OUT OF THE WAY . . .

Delegating authority and responsibility to an empowered team means blending appropriate individuals, skills, and coaching. The role of the manager is to create an imperative by communicating the needs outlined in the business plan in factual and substantive terms, indicating the constraints but stopping short of dictating the manner in which the team should behave. The latter remains the prerogative of the action team and will quickly crystallize as the team begins work to tackle the required improvement targets. Care must be taken, however, to avoid what one company discovered to be a downside to team empowerment. "To us it meant giving people guns but not giving them a common target to aim at," said one executive. "I guess we should not have been surprised when in the beginning some individuals began aiming at other members within the organization."

Well-trained teams create an informal system of control and develop operating procedures to govern the roles, conduct, and expectations of each member within the group. In the words of Gary Collyer, a manager at the British Margam facility of the American transmissions giant Borg Warner Automotive, "an action team with an opinion and no facts is just another team with an attitude." The social dynamics rely on the ability of the team to negotiate standard operating procedures that are measurable and repeatable. During this period, fact holders and gatekeepers tend to assume positions of expertise and assistance, sharing proven patterns of behavior, methods, and techniques drawn from experience and special training. The maintenance of a standards policy is therefore self-reinforcing. Out of it evolve systems that create a shared frame of reference, unity of response, and cohesion between the team members.

An example of the evolution of standards and procedures between a team and its suppliers is demonstrated by the television manufacturer Sony and its manufacturing facility in the United Kingdom. On this occasion the major emphasis was on the co-location of all the action team members in a single office space to coordinate and develop the international movement of materials. The company had established a plant to produce television sets for the fiercely competitive European market in 1974. However, because high levels of subcontracting practiced in Japan could not be replicated in Britain, the company faced a key competitive disadvantage. This led to the launching of a process-focused management system with teams addressing quality, cost, and delivery problems the company could expect to experience with suppliers that had no history of operating within a lean, just-in-time system or meeting the highly demanding needs of a Japanese television manufacturer.

During the early years, as the factory was built and production began to ramp up, local suppliers proved unreliable and the cause of many operational problems within the plant. As a buffer, the plant was forced to hold a costly average stock level of 51 days at the plant, while growing sales exerted pressure for increased manufacturing space. A secondary problem that also became evident was the poor quality of incoming goods and the need to manually sort and inspect all inbound materials. Quality, cost, and delivery processes needed to be improved radically if the plant was to gain European market share.

However, rather than switch sources, Sony decided to remain with the suppliers and create an action team to improve their performance. This resulted in a joint campaign to improve the quality reliability of purchased products and became known as the Zero Defects program. As a common frame of reference for all suppliers, improvements in quality were quickly understood to yield equally beneficial results for supplier and customer alike. Sony also instigated a supplier development program, led by the team, to equip suppliers with quality control skills and to coordinate the improvement of quality and delivery to the plant.

Such efforts helped fuel the company's rapid growth in the European market while realizing tremendous savings within the supply chain. Sony reduced inventory by over two-thirds, eliminated receiving and inspection of inbound goods, and developed just-in–time supply with companies that have proved they are capable of meeting stringent half-life performance targets. Indeed, the success of the efforts triggered the relocation of small production units of major suppliers to within an hour's drive of the plant. In turn, Sony awarded higher-volume products and extended the trading relationship with suppliers. The company also instituted a "milkround" system, in which representatives visit each supplier and bring the products from the end of the suppliers' production line to the point at which the product is needed in the assembly of the television set. Action teams have refined the quality and delivery processes to the point that there is a complete transparency between buyer and vendor. All information systems are linked electronically to create even higher levels of value-adding opportunities for both trading partners.

INDIVIDUAL DEVELOPMENT AND LEADERSHIP

If everyone on a team is aware of the objectives of the company and knows well the short-term targets to be achieved, it is possible for any one member to take on the role of leader. Having worked closely in training together and setting goals, the team members become virtually interchangeable as leaders. One benefit of this is that the team nominates its own leader. This does not preclude, as an option, an individual's being delegated formal decision-making authority by the process owner one level higher. Whatever the choice, the working design principle is to minimize external management interference while maximizing internal team freedom to act. But when conflicts of opinion arise that cannot be solved by the formal leader, arbitration can be sought from the process manager. Involving the process manager too often, however, is a sign that the team is not receiving sufficient information or has not recognized its level of authority.

❖ Having worked closely in training together and setting goals, the team members become virtually interchangeable as leaders.

Building a system in which action teams are accountable for the nuts and bolts of day-to-day business requires careful training and planning. Especially important is development of individual and team decision-making authority. This activity is the responsibility of the process manager. It calls for the provision of resources, technology, and additional people so that teams are continually being prepared for competitive success. This may include assignment of members to other areas to learn new skills or refresh existing ones. "Individuals in our teams are regularly rotated in order to spread the benefits of this approach throughout the organization," says Lyndon Jones, plant manager at Calsonic Llanelli Radiators, "and also to give the individual the opportunity to gain new skills and face new challenges in different environments and with different customers." However, because such skills and competencies are frequently undervalued and the training is seen as too costly in time and money, the capabilities of many action teams are blunted.

Traits of the Ideal Action Team

- A self-sufficient and highly motivated team can focus more effectively on business improvement.
- The ability to exploit the group's collective intelligence is enhanced.
- Decision making is pushed to the lowest possible level for accuracy and speed.
- The manager is released to plan for the future.
- Teams provide a collaborative forum that can make work more effective and enjoyable.
- Information flow between the manager and the teams ensures that business planning and review procedures are dynamic and centralized.
- Team efforts are more easily coordinated through "multiskilling" of individual team members so that the organization becomes highly flexible and adaptive.
- Collective learning of the team rapidly decreases the time required to master new challenges.
- The team establishes its own rules and assigns its own work.
- Each member is trained in problem-solving methods, allowing selection of the appropriate tool for the problem.
- There is greater acceptance of decisions taken by members, including the personal commitment of people who "buy into" the decision.
- Peer pressure is used to police the system without the need for management intervention.
- Individuals do not feel threatened when criticized, because individual competition is replaced by a common team focus.

It is a truism to say that "no individual comes to work to do a bad job," but a rather bad job is the result of not fully integrating the individual into the business. Action teams are the platforms through which process managers can delegate day-to-day operations. All this implies new behavior from the process manager given that substantial authority is delegated to teams. It means abandoning the temptation to fall back on functional specialization and the DAISY command mind-set. It is just such recurring temptations that can quickly undermine and even doom the efforts to build a lean, flexible organization.

NOTE

1. More information on the Lane Group's approach can be found in Nick Rich, *Partnering for Success: How Small- and Medium-Sized Firms Gain from Partnership Sourcing* (Partnership Sourcing, 1995).

PART III

Core
Processes

Chapter 10

CREATING NEW PRODUCTS

As with apparel makers, many stores have failed to keep up with the changes in women. Retailing is littered with the graves of merchants like I. Magnin, Petrie Stores and Merry-Go-Round. And stores that once seemed invulnerable—Ann Taylor Stores, Charivari, the Limited and Casual Corner, among them are deeply troubled.

"Fashion Relearns Basic Darwin: Be Adaptable or Be Extinct," *New York Times*, August 6, 1996.

C onceiving a new product or service is the lifeblood of a growth-minded business. Yet, because of the complexity involved in the innovation process, rarely is it the work of a single, cloistered genius. In most cases, a wide variety of activities and subsystems must be merged into a flawlessly operating whole. It can be as complex as designing an aircraft, with networks of 200 or more subteams totaling 10,000 people, or creating a new car platform with a team of 700 to 1,000 engineers, or as technically difficult as a new software solution involving perhaps millions of lines of code. What we have come to learn in the preceding chapters is that a fragmented, linear approach in which people work at arm's length is no longer possible. Too much is left to chance. There is redundancy of effort, errors crop up, and as time is lost market opportunities vanish. What then does "mastery" mean when treated as a whole process?

When the Trane Company, a division of American Standard, moved to a strategic process structure, one of its first acts was to name the process focused on product development. Mark Bergman, a division vice-president who "owns" the process, told about wrestling with the subject. "We have a product that has a long life and for us one of the biggest problems is the quick turnaround of small change orders. This is why we came up with the emphasis on product *change* and development." In his case, change orders require rapid response by manufacturing, which needs to alter tools and procedures, as well as the logistics staff, which must revise manuals and alert field offices and distributors of updates. Managing change orders gives the company a definite competitive advantage by meeting customer needs more quickly and effectively.

Over a period of four years, Bergman and eight program managers operated as a cross-organizational team intent on building an inventory of best practices propagated through product-focused action teams at the company's dispersed plant sites. "Whereas before we operated by the local experience and instincts of our best managers to try and coordinate separate functions around the development of new products," Bergman said, "we now meet and share practices in such a way that makes the coordination of our work more predictable." In short, by taking a process perspective, Trane is not only getting a handle on the management of its resources, but in a major shift in power the process owners now control their product development budgets, previously controlled by separate functional departments or plant managers.

Cincinnati Milacron, a global maker of machine tool systems was spurred into action in the late 1980s when faced with severe competition for its line of products, particularly from aggressive Japanese manufacturers. Central to its revival was the reengineering of its new product development process. This was largely done at a corporate level in the United States with the involvement of the regional manufacturing divisions spread across the globe. At the time, poor quality was costing the firm 30 percent of its turnover. In the British factory alone, 750 suppliers had to be to dealt with one-on-one. Given such hurdles, it took Cincinnati Milacron four to five years to bring a new product to market. The U.K. manufacturing director, Mike Ryan, recalled:

> "If we were to survive as a manufacturing force and maintain a good level of employment at Birmingham, we needed to do things differently, and we also needed to offer our employees the tools, in terms of management strategy, to enable them to be successful and to do things differently. We needed a new product range. We needed the ability for fast production ramp-up because the one thing we didn't have on our side was time."

To effect such changes Cincinnati Milacron instituted a lean process-focused approach and coined a nickname for it: Wolfpack. The purpose was to cut the fat from the organization, optimize its processes, and fine-tune its agility in response to market demands. As Ryan explained, in a rather cold-blooded metaphor, "Wolves are known to hunt in packs, and we see simultaneous engineering teams in our various divisions as a pack. Wolves look after, work together, and support each other, and wolves eventually destroy their opposition." To do this the company instituted a companywide process team with representatives from sales and marketing, design engineering, production engineering, quality, inventory control, parts manufacturing, assembly, finance, field service, electronic systems, and shipping. In the initial stages most of the team worked full-time on the project. In the first few weeks they analyzed market needs, developed the basic concept, and drew up an implementation program. After that only the leader continued full-time, with other specialists brought in as required. However, the whole team still met every two weeks to review progress right through to the time of actual production.

Below the companywide process team, four action teams were used for purchasing, manufacturing, costing, and design. The manufacturing team, for example, was led by an engineer. This team continually assessed the designs being developed by the main project team. The members focused on such questions as whether the design would cause the problems in manufacturing. They reviewed tolerances, size, and variety of parts, as well as whether existing facilities were suitable. The purchasing team ensured the early involvement of suppliers at design briefings. Ryan elaborated, "The suppliers have the opportunity to tell us where we are likely to give them difficulties and where we could save money by letting them do something at a lower cost. We develop very close supplier relationships, of whom there are now just 60, down from 750."

Although there was a modicum of initial project manager training, the success of the working innovations lay in two areas. First was top management's commitment to the process, and second was the outstanding success of the first product developed. Ryan commented, "If the commitment comes from the top down, you have a very good chance of making it work." In Cincinnati Milacron's case, it was the managing director who launched the simultaneous engineering process in the firm. He was convinced of its usefulness and convinced other senior managers.

❖ "If the commitment comes from the top down, you have a very good chance of making it work."

Since adopting this new strategy and approach, the company's British site has cut product development from one and a half years in the first model to one year in the second and to a total of one and a half years for models three, four, and five together. This is far from a one-shot success. In the United States, a Cincinnati Milacron plastic injection molding machine facility using similar methods has reduced new product development lead time by half, increased the functionality of the product, and reduced the cost by 40 percent. The result: In the first full year of production, the company sold two and a half times as many of the new machines as it had in the best year of the earlier model. Behind such successes is tangible evidence that the top-level strategy process team at Cincinnati Milacron is focusing new product development innovation effectively worldwide.

TACKLING LONG-STANDING PROBLEMS

The problem with the traditional product change and development process is that there rarely *is* a process. In too many companies product development falls under the tutelage of a single department. According to Massachusetts Institute of Technology professor and former Xerox principal engineer Don Clausing, "Product development is very easy. But we have made it very hard for cultural reasons. It should be one system, one team, one set of decisions."[1]

Another problem is that the product change and development process is typically undervalued. It is often the first activity to be cut back when nonessential corporate restructuring occurs. Yet, in the best organizations it is given center stage and everybody reacts accordingly. The reason for this is that world-class firms such as Cincinnati Milacron and others have come to accept certain factual marketplace inevitabilities:

Fact. As consumer tastes become more varied and individualistic, it is necessary to produce a greater range of products.

Fact. In fast-moving markets, the first company to bring a new product to market reaps the greater initial profit, often by being able to charge premium prices that later drop as others enter the market. Latecomers can be left with slim margins and costly marketing programs.

Fact. As lean companies perfect their manufacturing skills, lower defect rates, and improve delivery times, new product development remains one of the key areas where competitive advantage can still be gained.

THE SEARCH FOR BEST PRACTICES

In early 1990, when the International Association for Product Development (IAPD) was cofounded by Dan Dimancescu to identify best practices worldwide, the new product development process in Western firms was under fire. Various academic leaders were condemning it for its lack of discipline and for inefficient methods. This was typified in the Harvard Business School work of Professors Kim

Clark and Takahiro Fujimoto, who showed that cars made in the United States took nearly twice as long to design as those made in Japan.[2] In addition, the Japanese manufacturing process was around a third faster.

Writers such as James Womack, Daniel Jones, and Daniel Roos, in the now classic management book *The Machine That Changed the World,* suggested that the Japanese focus on lean production might be superior to the traditional Western approach.[3] They pinpointed key areas where the Japanese were winning out in their product development: leadership, teamwork, communications, and simultaneous development. They concluded that, "taken together, lean techniques in these four areas make it possible to do a better job faster with less effort."

In collaboration with the IAPD in the United States, a similar six-company best-practice network was created in Wales in 1992 under a Welsh Development Agency initiative. The purpose of the joint Time to Market network was for leading companies on both sides of the Atlantic to discover, learn, and swap best practices. In time, ten key differentiating best practices were identified that together served to mobilize the intelligence of the workforce in creating new streams of products.[4]

Organizational Features and Process Enablers

- A three-tier process–based structure
- Cross–company teaming
- Performance–gap metrics
- Rewards and recognition
- Suppliers as partners
- Three-track technology management
- Four fields 'relationship' mapping
- Capturing the voice of the customer
- Rigorous gates and design reviews
- Shared-knowledge systems

Will Hill, a vice-president responsible for redesigning the organizational structure surrounding product development at Black &

Decker, recalled, "We started in the early 1990s with a very traditional functional development organization. It had all the expected departmental names at the top: mechanical design, electrical engineering, model shop, and so forth." These departments assigned staff to projects along the old matrix, two-boss system. The project team members had little control and were always looking over their shoulder at their respective functional heads. To break this hold, a new structure with unified operations within a teaming organization was set up, with project teams made answerable to a global business unit team.

The new project teams own the development resources in each of four product categories. They are supported, in turn, by competencies—not functions—in three strategically important areas: core technologies, such as batteries and motors; technical competencies; and other functions, including marketing, manufacturing, finance, and purchasing. "This system," said Hill, "empowers the leaders of teams. We have imposed a lot more structure when it comes to setting objectives and in learning how to control the process. The real difference here is that we have gotten away from the single (functional) boss saying 'do this.' "

One of the first to advocate the use of cross-functional teaming in the new product development process was Jay Galbraith, who in the 1970s argued for the building of lateral links within large companies. "Because lateral processes decentralize general management," he argued, "they free up top management for other decisions."[5] This theme was further developed by Ian Morley,[6]

1. Select cohesive teams.
2. Bring specialists from all major functional areas.
3. Ensure a common vision.
4. Organize controlled convergence in solution resolution.
5. Encourage open-minded thinking.
6. Maintain a balance between individual and group work.
7. Use systemic methods.
8. Use formal and informal communication.

9. Select members according to their aptitudes to the particular work at hand.
10. Provide strong leadership and encourage team empowerment.

These ten teaming principles are critical to successful new product development within the three-tier system of management. Also important is the linking of different complementary R&D efforts. Japanese TV maker Sharp does this by employing Gold Badge Teams, which are responsible for bringing products to the market in the fastest possible way. These fast-track teams integrate proven technologies generated by Sharp's laboratories into the highest-priority new product lines, bypassing the usual diffusion of technology from research laboratories to product development. These teams are empowered by the president and wear the same gold badge he wears to signify their priority status. A team typically stays in place for about two years and is given priority on personnel.[7]

Another significant feature of successful new product development is the involvement of suppliers. In 1991, plant manager Lyndon Jones at Calsonic's Llanelli Radiators in Wales brought together a group of nine key suppliers in an unprecedented supplier association (see Chapter 12) to focus as a group on automotive cooling needs at Calsonic. After some trepidation Jones told the suppliers, "My foremost intent is to improve the new product development and I can't do that without you, and you can't do it without us only letting you in early on the new product development process." A few seconds of disbelieving silence followed, broken by a managing director of one of the suppliers, who said, "I've been telling you that for years, but how are you going to do that?" Jones, who had anticipated the query, retorted, "That's why I've brought you together—so you can decide." This one step set into motion a radical improvement in new product development at Calsonic Llanelli Radiators.

The early involvement of suppliers is helping to shatter past management practice. When brought into the process late, as was the norm, suppliers could only respond to designs already in place at the client company. The only way to compete in such circumstances was on the basis of the lowest quoted cost. Addressing this point, former Xerox principal engineer Don Clausing commented, "This led to a proliferation of a company's suppliers, none of whom were contributing significantly to the design of new products. As a result," he added, "designs were often ill suited to the capabilities of suppliers."[8] The move toward process-based new product development with early supplier involvement, therefore, translates into fewer suppliers. Clausing confirmed that at Xerox the introduction of such an approach led to a reduction in suppliers from more than 3,000 in the early 1980s to fewer than 400 in the late 1980s. This decrease allowed more strategic relationships to be developed with fewer core firms. On the same topic, Jim Currier, vice-president of purchasing at NCR, argued, "Our chances of bringing innovative solutions to the marketplace will depend on our suppliers; one can't simply afford to 'own' all the requisite technology needed to satisfy customer expectations."[9]

USER NEEDS: THE ACHILLES HEEL OF PRODUCT DEVELOPMENT

The application of process-management practices has been particularly important in mastering the critical front end of the product development process, the zone of activity most prone to radical improvement in Western companies. This high-leverage zone includes the preconcept and early product definition stages. More recently, various downstream concerns such as environmental impacts and product obsolescence have become increasingly important. In these areas European companies such as BMW, with its auto "unbuilding factories," and U.K. homecare retailer B&Q, with its strict product environmental care charter, are leading the way.

Edith Wilson, a manager on the corporate staff at Hewlett-Packard set out in 1990 to determine the causes behind product development failures and successes. Studying about thirty cases within the company, she uncovered twelve factors common to all projects. One stood out as more important than the others: "understanding of user needs" topped the scale as most likely to cause failure if not enacted. This insight led the company to design new ways of capturing user needs. "We did this," said Wilson, "but also strengthened the product definition through a studied attention to each of the twelve factors. This stage is critical since it is the starting point for what creates real value to HP's business."

A thorough understanding of what customers actually want from a product is now widely recognized as crucial to the success of a new product. Attaining that understanding is often a trial-and-error journey of discovery. A U.K.-based washing machine manufacturer came to understand the limitations of what were once viewed as state-of-the-art techniques for probing customer needs. It had constructed a test laboratory for washers inside a room with two-way mirrors. It then invited actual and potential customers to try out the machines with their dirty laundry. The exercise proved very useful. However, one of the marketers noted that he did not think they were getting close enough to reality. "Surely," he said, "we should test the product in real surroundings when the people using them have all the distractions, noises, smells, interruptions, and hassles of normal housework."

He was, of course, right. This was a lessons that Yogesh Parikh of Digital Equipment had learned some years before. A team is used in that company with a small number of key clients—generally ones who are willing to risk buying new products—who are termed "lead users" or "early adopters." They spend an extended amount of time observing how the clients work and the role a particular product plays in that work environment. This system of contextual inquiry gives Digital "a far better vision of the system," said Parikh, "by seeing the working links between an individual, his group, and his organization. A clear picture of work structures, work concepts, work intentions, and work outputs is gained, which can then be tied to a system structure, system concepts, functionality, and system artifacts."

THE CASE OF THE RETURNING DIGGERS

A well-known manufacturer of mechanical backhoes was having a major problem. Its new hoes kept being returned with bent axles. "That is impossible," remarked the frustrated design engineer; "for the new model, the axle specifications are far higher than those of our competitors, and there's no way they could bend in normal operation." He came up with the only possible cause: "It must be mistreatment by our customers."

After several months, and several dozen returns, one of the young secretaries, fed up with typing letters of placation to the customers, suggested going to see the product actually being used. "Then we'll know the cause of the problem," she said. Common sense won out. A small team (including the secretary) was put together, and an off-the-record visit was arranged to a local farmer known to favor the company's product.

The team spent the morning watching him dig ditches, move earth, and unclog waterways. Nothing seemed amiss. After lunch, he started to clear some tree stumps. After the farmer spent half an hour fixing the special stump puller to the back of the hoe and another half-hour pulling up two large stumps, the manufacturing company team decided to leave the farmer to his work and phone back to the office to report a wasted day. However, the secretary hid behind some bushes to watch. Seeing the crowd leave, the farmer was greatly relieved because he could now double his work rate by knocking the stumps out like usual.

This procedure consisted of taking a thirty-foot run at a stump and jerking it out with the stump-pulling equipment still attached to his digger. The secretary recorded the farmer doing this six or seven times before the stump came loose. When the rest of the team returned to tell her that they were going back to the office, she reported her discovery. The design engineer quickly retorted, "I told you these guys are misusing the equipment."

"Not at all," replied the secretary; "it's just that you didn't design it for how they wanted to use it." After some discussion on the way home the design engineer had to admit that the secretary had a point. Although he wasn't ready to admit it publicly, he decided to make sure that the next new product took into account the exact user needs, not his best guess of them. And he did. The next new product was awarded Britain's premier design award, the prestigious Design Council British Design Award for Innovation.

Note: This case is loosely based on a true story recounted by a member of the Welsh Time-to-Market network.

KEEPING TEAMS FOCUSED AND PRODUCTIVE

While many of the most successful new product developers have adopted or are adopting a three-tier styled management system to achieve excellence in product development, a few are devising control systems that measure whether the process is working. One of these companies is Hewlett-Packard.

In the 1990s the Hewlett-Packard computer peripheral division in Bristol, England, established itself as a market leader in digital audiotape technology used for computer backup. During this time five products have been launched with a continuous reduction in Time-to-Market (TTM) achieved. The last two improvement cycles have seen this time halved.

This resulted from a specific TTM program launched in 1990 designed to develop both management and technical processes. The program revolved around cross-functional teams led by program managers. The aim was to create a dynamic "small business" culture. Because Hewlett-Packard realized that both the management and the technical processes were critical, it set out to conduct "postmortems" in both of these areas. It wanted to know what did and did not work. This was done using two-day workshops bringing together managers from the functional areas who had direct responsibility within the past program. Also, two program managers for future development were invited as customers of the workshop's output. The internal technical objective was to "repeat the good stuff for the next programs and to improve on the not-so-good stuff the next time around."

A combination of cartoon depictions of other functional groups, mapping each other's needs, and discussing the outputs led to a creative mix of good fun, good practices, and targeted areas for development and improvement. Following this, the team worked on the key priority area until improvements had been designed and implemented. One such improvement was the addition of two phases in the design process reinforcing and strengthening the "fuzzy" front end of product definition, realizing a 70 percent time reduction in this area and a 40 percent reduction in terms of overall cycle time. It is no coincidence that Hewlett-Packard is now regarded as one of the world's best product definers.

Another innovative company is Italian domestic appliance producer Zanussi. Its application of science to the new product development process involves the use of ten separate metrics or metric sets. These measurements encompass three kinds of performance areas: cost, quality, and time. These data are collected weekly and summarized in a monthly reporting structure. The data collection allows for both a time series collection of information, such as the cost of the complete TTM process as well as the respective cost, quality, and time in any part of the process, such as the product planning phase.

By sustaining a system of product development process measurement such as Zanussi's, a company can, in effect, monitor its rate of learning much in the manner of the half-life curves introduced in Chapter 5. Learning is reflected in a process team's ability to reduce strategically important performance gaps consistently over time. But measurement alone is hardly a panacea. Cohesive teaming that involves open and frequent interaction, well-focused direction setting, and a keen sense of what it takes to identify user needs demonstrate complementary aspects of effective core process management. Rigorous review methods and judicious oversight by senior management ensure that the business case is not sacrificed to cost overruns, misunderstandings of user expectations, errors, or time delays.

NOTES

1. The best summary of Don Clausing's work can be found in *Total Quality Development: A Step-By-Step Guide to World-Class Concurrent Engineering* (New York: ASME Press, 1994).
2. Kim Clark and Takahiro Fujimoto, *Product Development Performance: Strategy, Organization, and Management in the World Auto Industry* (Boston, Mass.: Harvard Business Press, 1991).
3. James Womack, Daniel Jones, and Daniel Roos, *The Machine That Changed the World* (New York: Rawson Associates, 1990).
4. See Dan Dimancescu and Kemp Dwenger, *World-Class New Product Development* (New York: AMACOM, 1996).
5. Jay Galbraith, *Designing Organizations* (Reading, Mass.: Addison Wesley, 1995).
6. Ian Morley, "Building Cross-Functional Design Teams," *Proceedings of the First International Conference on Integrated Design Management,* London, 1990, pp. 100–110.
7. Lewis Branscomb and Fumio Kodama, *Japanese Innovation Strategy: Technical Support for Business Visions* (Lanham, Md.: University Press of America, 1993).
8. Clausing, *Total Quality Development.*
9. "Design Report: Part I," *Purchasing,* February 8, 1990, p. 47.

Chapter 11

"THE ORDER IS LATE"

I decided one day to ask our key executives: "If the phone rang today and you picked it up, what is the most likely message you would get?" The answer was, "The order is late." I knew right away that we had a very serious problem.

Ray Stata, founder and chairman of
Analog Devices

How well a company delivers a customer order, on time, undamaged, and in the right quantity, can make or break that company. Some, like L. L. Bean, the famed dry-goods retailer headquartered in a small town in Maine, built a vast and highly profitable mail order business based on prompt and flawless overnight shipments. Its efficient ways helped set a world-class standard emulated by many in various other industries. For others, like Analog Devices, a failure to attend to the delivery needs of its customers—in this case for highly sophisticated semiconductors— got it into trouble. During the middle 1980s, it discovered that its most critical customer had done a most embarrassing thing. In the lobby of Hewlett-Packard's Palo Alto, California, vendor offices were two prominently displayed panels. One, to the left, listed the corporation's ten best customers. To the right another listed the ten worst. And, yes, to its dismay, Analog Devices was at the bottom of the right-hand side. That story, of course, has a happy ending, for

Analog Devices climbed back to the top of the left-hand side by attending aggressively to the management of its order fulfillment process. Order fulfillment is considerably more complex than just putting a product onto a truck and making sure it arrives at the appointed hour. At Analog Devices it means controlling the production of semiconductors and ensuring high yields of flawless chips.

A more modest example of gaining control over the order fulfillment process is that of Trico Australia, a maker of windshield wipers owned by the Stant Corporation in the United States. It was realized, as a senior executive put it, that "we would have been out of business had we not done something radical." As a result of a process-driven strategy, the company not only survived but prospered during a period in which foreign competition increased (particularly from Japan), tariff protection declined, and a major recession seriously affected the Australian economy.

A visitor to Trico Australia's facilities in 1990 would have found it hard not to be impressed by its just-in-time (JIT) manufacturing. All the key features were apparent: one-piece flow, and on lights, quick setup times, short lead times, and a *kanban* system (in which a worker on a production line calls for replenishment of materials as needed, thus ensuring that the flow of supplies corresponds to the need at the right time and in the right amount). Because the shop-floor employees had been systematically consulted, there had been strong support for the ensuing five-year trek to mastering JIT. However, Trico Australia's executive team knew that more was necessary. There were still many problems and difficulties. What was really called for was a workforce that abandoned a narrow task-based view of work and could grasp the larger impact of the work any one individual did. In short, how could they make operators realize that the way they had been doing their job for the last twenty years was probably not the correct way?

❖ How could they make operators realize that the way they had been doing their job for the last twenty years was probably not the correct way?

The first step occurred with the formation in 1990 of a team to find ways in which critical work, such as order fulfillment, could be treated as a single companywide process. The initial top-level team consisted of the managing director, operations director, and company secretary, with key managers drawn from sales, purchasing, marketing, manufacturing, and quality. It also included representatives from the shop floor and even the union. They all had a part to play in rethinking the way in which work could be more effectively managed.

The members met fortnightly to discuss a variety of issues, including teamwork, the concept of leaders rather than managers, and the skills required in the new organization. It also tackled how goals could be established and accountability assigned within future work teams. Everything from mission to strategy, from process to individual behavior was up for grabs. This top-level team paved the way for the Trico Restructuring Improvement Program that yielded an easy-to-remember acronym: TRIP. Out of this would be born a three-tier system of management. When the first restructuring pilots took place in 1991 in the blade manufacturing area, however, there were only two team levels—the senior planning group and an implementation work team. Things did not flow as expected. Despite the careful planning, initial efforts were less than successful. In fact, if anything, things slipped backward. One of the reasons was management's unrealistic expectations. The second was that the action teams were left largely to fend for themselves, a failing common to many change efforts. No one had given thought to the intense training needed to slowly cultivate different behavior and new attitudes toward work, careers, and colleagues.

❖ Despite the careful planning, initial efforts were less than successful. In fact, if anything, things slipped backward. One of the reasons was management's unrealistic expectations.

Shortly afterward, a middle support tier of three cross-organizational groups was put in place between the larger planning group and a wider span of work teams (see Figure 11.1). Each support group consisted of 10–12 team leaders from each of three relevant process areas and other pertinent staff from engineering, sales, and manufacturing. This ensured a close link between the support group and the individual work teams below them. A similar link was created with one planning group member serving on each support group.

This new organizational architecture—not task- or function-based—made cross-organizational communication faster and greatly increased flexibility within the company. In addition, everyone in the company became more focused on the product and the customers' requirements. One consequence is that communication in the company is through no more than two operating layers. To further aid information flow, the managing director gives quarterly feedback to all team members. Information is also shared through a weekly news sheet called "Trico Rumors" and a quarterly magazine called *Trip-In around Trico*.

❖ This new organizational architecture—not task- or function-based—made cross-organizational communication faster and greatly increased flexibility within the company.

By 1994, eleven support teams became parent to a total of thirty-five work teams with an average membership of six employees. In addition, the support teams were periodically assisted by impromptu working groups focused on specific tasks and disbanded

11.1. Design for Trico Australia's work teams.

Planning Group		
Support Group Linkage Area	Support Group Blade Area	Support Group Arm Area
Work Team 1 Work Team 2	Work Team 1 Work Team 2 Work Team 3 Work Team 4	Work Team 1 Work Team 2

when the task was complete. Work flexibility within the groups allowed quicker responses in answer to customer changes in volume deliveries, tooling alterations, and design changes. Worker acceptance of the new teaming approach was partly manifested in negligible employee turnover and absenteeism and partly in a doubling of productivity per worker. Trico Australia's reputation ascended accordingly into that of a highly reliable and consistent supplier. Sales quadrupled.[1]

A COMPANY'S SUCCESS WITH THREE-TIER PROCESS

One of the first companies to use the three-tier strategic process approach was JUKI's Industrial Sewing Machine Division, awarded the prestigious Deming Prize in 1981, only two years after it embarked on a major change program. JUKI was led by a hard-driving former naval officer. Throughout the company, evidence of "lessons learned from defeat in war" are parceled about. It is not unexpected, therefore, to find mission statements focused on winning, much as one would express winning a battle. To arrive at this goal, JUKI's key to success—other than a keen understanding of its technology and its customers' needs—was a simple process–driven strategy aimed at excelling in its coordination of cross–company activities.

At the top, the senior-level team, called the Executive Management Committee, is charged with the responsibility of making improvements in each of its key companywide processes, of which delivery is one of a handful. Best practices could thus be shared between process areas to address problems, and resource needs could be better balanced between the four process-owning teams. Each of these teams is given performance gap targets by the Executive Management Committee, and the progress is monitored quarterly. The Delivery Control Team is responsible for order fulfillment. Its mandate is to sustain continual improvement in the performance of order fulfillment by JUKI. This long-term emphasis sustains steady streams of improvement that eventually generate a half-life rate of improvement. This is not a one-shot "SWAT" executive team more familiar to Western companies. Instead, a permanent expectation is created that every year will yield improvement. The team's role is to design a process necessary to master order fulfillment, to assign action teams to carry out specific tasks, and to monitor and check those actions so that the process itself can be improved.

❖ This is not a one-shot "SWAT" executive team more familiar to Western companies. Instead, a permanent expectation is created that every year will yield improvement.

11.2. Three-tier management at JUKI.

Tier One:
Executive Management Team

Tier Two: Strategic Processes

| Delivery Control Team | Profit/Cost Management Team | New Product Development Team | Quality Team |

Tier Three: Action Teams (e.g., within the Delivery Control Team)

| Human Resource Development | Targeted Methods | Prerequisite Improvement Methods | Standards Promotion |

At the third tier of work, within the domain of the Delivery Control Team, action-minded teams identify and prioritize short-term measures necessary to narrow a critical performance gap, such as delivery time. Four such measures were put into operation. The Human Resource Development Team, for example, works on identifying the skills necessary for employees to undertake improvements and on finding ways of bridging any gaps. Other teams identify and implement new process methods, reduce lead times, and standardize results across the organization (see Figure 11.2). The functional departments then collaborate in carrying out specific activities. The whole cycle is repeated annually. At JUKI some of the order fulfillment activities chosen for special attention include:

- Improving sales-forecasting methods
- Improving the order entry system
- Coordinating sales and manufacturing more closely
- Leveling manufacturing flow
- Reducing planning and manufacturing lead times
- Reorganizing the parts management system
- Synchronizing purchasing and manufacturing
- Optimizing inventory holding levels
- Adopting a *kanban* system with suppliers

In the words of one JUKI senior executive, the secret behind the companywide process management success lies in "the periodic evaluation of activities, vigorous analysis, and continuous improvement efforts." The result of a decade and a half of these improvement efforts is evident in JUKI's preeminence in its industry.[2]

ORDER FULFILLMENT IN A SMALLER COMPANY

Can the three-tier system of management be used by the smaller company, or is it just for huge corporations? The answer can be found at Q8 Lubricants, an industrial lubricant factory located in Leeds, the industrial heartland of England and one of the earliest centers of mass production in the world.

Leeds is a principal city in the county of Yorkshire, a county that is famous for many achievements, not least the excellence of its cricketers. Cricket is a sport that baffles most American visitors to the British Isles, in much the same way that the British fail to understand the complex strategic plays of American baseball. The sporting excellence of individuals and teams in such areas as cricket is typical of most activities undertaken by Yorkshire men and women and is easily transferred to the industrial context.

The Q8 lubricant plant is the British manufacturing facility of oils for engine and machining applications and is owned by the Kuwait Petroleum Corporation, one of the largest petroleum refining companies in the world. Therefore, the Leeds plant belongs to a much larger, worldwide family of manufacturing and converting sites. In terms of its position in the family, however, it is one of the most respected and favored facilities, holding many awards for the excellence of its products. In a recent benchmarking survey of lubricant manufacturers in Europe, Q8 was awarded the leading position in the United Kingdom and the number four position in all of Europe. These figures represent quite an achievement for this small facility so many miles from the Kuwaiti oil fields, the source of its materials.

The manufacturing plant itself is located on an old industrial estate on the outskirts of Leeds behind a grove of tall trees. The only sign of the company's presence is the two large flags displaying the distinctive logo of the corporation as they flutter gently in the breeze. Once you are through the entrance, the sleepy first impressions of the industrial estate are replaced by a hive of activity.

The Q8 lubricant plant is a particularly "shy" facility and management does not tend to boast of its many achievements, preferring to show a resolve to do better today than yesterday. In the reception area, visitors are greeted with a characteristic cheerful welcome and presented with a mandatory cup of coffee. Archie Dempster, head of manufacturing and quality at the plant, soon trots down the stairs and with a powerful handshake personally welcomes visitors. Indeed, Dempster refers to the facility as his "baby" and displays the fondness of a father for his firstborn child.

Dempster is a well-known figure in the European lubricant industry. The company's vision he has imparted for the past few years has been to develop an entire organization with a mission. This mission is to be world class in all aspects of operation and to make every minute of every day count in converting lubricants from raw materials to finished products that are displayed center stage on many merchandisers' shelves. It seems unusual that a senior business manager such as Dempster should talk in terms of minutes rather than pounds sterling, but to Dempster each member of his team has 480 minutes available in a single day, and it is each worker's job to ensure that this finite resource is spent wisely. Managing in minutes is a daunting method of self-analysis and provides understanding of just how an individual spends his or her day.

The measurement of all company activities in minutes reflects Dempster's desire to manufacture orders just in time for their delivery. In his view, it takes only five minutes to fill an automobile with engine oil. Therefore, the ideal lubricant facility would replenish that bottle of oil only minutes after it has been sold. A major focus of Dempster's strategic planning has been to discourage a feeling of overconfidence because of the awards the company has won and instead develop an organization of people who are dedicated to banishing waste from the company. To Dempster, people are the key to creating the ideal lubricant factory.

❖ It takes only five minutes to fill an automobile with engine oil. Therefore, the ideal lubricant facility would replenish that bottle of oil only minutes after it has been sold.

The effects of this commitment could be seen when one of Dempster's management team, Andy Dixon, took charge of the distribution channels of the company. Dixon had worked with Dempster for several years, starting on the filling lines of the facility. Through dedication to the company he had taken night courses that helped in his promotion to the position of logistics manager. Understanding the need to ensure interaction between the customer and the order fulfillment department of the Leeds plant, Dixon soon created a team to implement the distribution channels that would be needed to sustain the ideal facility. As part of this process, it was decided that distribution of the company's products should be handled by a company that specialized in logistics services. Successfully concluding the deal with the third party had major ramifications for the development of the Leeds factory of the future.

The new partnership between the two organizations meant that the products of the company would be managed effectively and efficiently as a joint venture, the logistician providing the distribution excellence demanded by the company and the Q8 lubricant plant managing the order fulfillment. At this time in the history of the company and its reorganization, the British headquarters, operated by Kuwait Petroleum (Great Britain), and the London international office (Kuwait Petroleum International), had joined forces to sponsor an industrial research program led by a university team from Cardiff and Bath. This research involved understanding and implementing lean principles across the enterprise.

The academic work was carried out by authors Peter Hines and Nick Rich within a supply chain development program, sponsored in part by eighteen of Europe's leading supply chain management companies from the food, retail, automotive, electronics, clothing, service, and process industries. All of the firms had a desire to be world class and to work with the academic research team to find innovative solutions to help them do this. (Hines acts as a program director and Rich as a program manager for the work at the Lean Enterprise Research Centre.)

The initial visits by Hines and Rich included an introduction at the two headquarters that provided an overview of the company operations. During the visit, it was suggested by Neil Harding-Deans, purchasing manager of Kuwait Petroleum (Great Britain), that Hines and Rich visit the Leeds facility to understand the lubricant business.

When the researchers arrived, they enjoyed the warm welcome and cup of coffee followed by an invitation to the boardroom, where Dempster and his team were waiting. In his own energetic presentation style, Dempster outlined the strategic direction of the business and an appreciation of the rich history of the facility. It was not long before he was detailing the operations and how they should be directed for the future. Before anyone had produced business cards, Dempster had arranged a tour of the facility so the researchers could see "the baby" in operation. After about an hour the team reconvened in the boardroom and began to discuss the performance of the plant and the mission to be world class.

By day's end the discussions had left no aspect of the company's operations untouched. The by-now-exhausted researchers were allowed to retire to a local hotel. The next day, the ritual continued, with coffee and a viselike welcoming hand from Dempster, but this time he stopped and fired the direct question at his guests, "What shall we do in the factory today?" Without waiting for an answer, he followed with the second question, "How are you going to support our drive for world class?" Stopping for a moment, Dempster smiled to himself and issued the instruction that no person could understand how the factory should operate in the future without spending time with the people who would drive the system.

Without further delay, Dempster had reached for the factory intercom, and after a short while one of the plant team leaders appeared. Greeting the team leader, Dempster demanded, "Show them how the factory works. And treat them like any other process operator." He turned and left.

Unsure as to who the visitors were but willing to trust Dempster's judgment, the team leader took Hines and Rich to the production floor and introduced them to the local action team members. The first stopping point in the tour was at the soluble plant, so called because the oil is mixed with water to form fluids for industrial machining purposes. After meeting the team from there, the group progressed to the "neat" plant, which derives its name from the blending of oil and additives without the need for water. These grades of lubricant are used in the production of engine oils. Both the plants are large and stand many meters high and combine to produce many millions of liters of oil each year.

The next stage of the tour progressed to the filling lines, where blended product is pumped to machines that fill plastic bottles and drums with the final product. These lines are divided between the frantic speeds achieved by the semiautomated lines, filling plastic bottles, to the more labor-intensive filling of 205-liter drums. Following the process through, the team arrived at reception once more and returned to the boardroom.

The assembled personnel discussed the factory's future and the outcome of exploiting the advantages offered by the third-party logistician. To identify the next stage of the factory's development and the extent of progress toward world-class status, the visitors proposed a series of "value stream" mapping tools and discussed their application within the plant.[3]

After a preliminary analysis of the tools, beginning with the line operators and managers, some issues began to surface. The production of materials in large batches created a surplus of materials in the distribution system. The flow of production batches was then slowed down because previous batches had to be processed first in the queue. Finally, the unnecessary inventory thus created in the system added to the number of minutes the materials were in the factory being converted. These interrelated areas would be used to focus short-term attention in the factory on eliminating sources of waste, especially wasted time, measured in minutes. Throughout the initial program, the effort was to be on distinguishing between those factors that absorbed the company's resources wastefully and those that truly added value to customers. After a few short weeks the Q8 staff was presented with the following findings:

1. There were some delays in the flow of materials through the manufacturing and logistics systems.
2. The facility required re-layout to meet the optimum flow of materials.
3. Procedures required standardization and streamlining.
4. Large batches were hiding possible improvement areas.
5. Actual customer demand was masked by stocks held in the logistics system.

These conclusions were filtered out of a series of traditional industrial engineering tools, an aspect that pleased Dempster because he had used such tools as an engineering apprentice. Enthusiasm grew as the presentation slides began to paint a picture of the future factory, including a route map for the achievement of this plan.

As the feedback continued, the management team was introduced to new tools drawn from other areas, such as logistics. These were used to support the main industrial engineering drive and exploit the power of a good logistics network and the capabilities of the plant. At the end of the feedback session the team was eager to understand the sources of and solutions to some of the plant's inefficiencies. An interest in exposing weaknesses is an almost universal sign of superior management ability and the relentless pursuit of perfection. This feature mirrors the experiences of companies such as Toyota and other exemplars. In the case of the Q8 lubricant plant, this passion for excellence is combined with a humble attitude toward congratulations. Dempster is more likely to retort, "We may be good but we need to be perfect" than to slap everyone on the back.

❖ An interest in exposing weaknesses is an almost universal sign of superior management ability and the relentless pursuit of perfection.

The result of the meeting was the formulation of a project to be used as a springboard to launch the company into its next stage of evolution as the world's leading lubricant manufacturer (see Figure 11.3). Very few planning meetings followed, but in the tradition of the plant, it was time to "walk the talk." The initial activity was to change the infrastructure of the plant and reassign individuals to key business processes. This was achieved quickly, and to complement the management team a group of five long-serving key personnel were placed in new positions of leadership throughout the plant. These people would "build" the new plant.

Once in place, the new action team leaders started to identify areas for improvement and the creation of a companywide solution to each area in turn. It soon became obvious that there was no long-term competitive advantage to be gained by retaining the machinery operated by the company; this type of filling and blending machinery could be purchased anywhere in the world. Neither were the products and formulations the key to success; they could be analyzed in any laboratory in the world. Competitive advantage could only be gained by harnessing the creative and innovative spirit of the personnel at the Leeds site. To do this required a new structure and a commitment to developing action teams to make improvements and sustain them. The company's version of the three-tier system was then created and plans were established to build upon the existing strengths and capabilities of the blending, filling, and logistics opera-

11.3. The improvement plan at the Q8 lubricant plant.

Short-term (0–6 months)

    Analyze lost production in minutes.
    Concentrate on improving order fulfillment in minutes.
    Review delivery performance of vendors.
    Review factory layout.
    Develop the interface between the company and the
        logistics network.

Medium-term (6–12 months)

    Introduce changes to align the process areas in the business.
    Develop performance-monitoring devices.
    Develop staff capabilities.
    Standardize company procedures.
    Implement changes to production facility.

Long-term (12 months onward)

    Synchronize the entire materials-to-distribution network.
    Develop staff skills.
    Develop new world-class performance gaps.
    Involve and develop the performance of suppliers.
    Seek new challenges.

---

tions of the facility. Once the system was developed, teams were briefed in detail to ensure that the message was deployed throughout the business.

❖ Competitive advantage could only be gained by harnessing the creative and innovative spirit of the personnel.

Having designed and constructed the means of implementing change focusing on order fulfillment, the researchers left the site, not expecting to see radical changes in their next visit because Q8 was already considered number one in the United Kingdom. Nothing could have been further from the truth. Within a month the factory had changed beyond recognition.

When Hines and Rich returned, the plant seemed unfamiliar. The building had not changed, except for new flags and a sign that proudly proclaimed the plant to be the home of Q8 lubricants, but something seemed different. Dempster, the management team, and the plant teams had literally turned the internal operations upside down in their search for added value and the removal of waste.

Once the researchers were inside, the changes became obvious. As cups of coffee were sipped, passing employees stopped to comment on how their areas had changed and also to apologize that they had not quite completed the plan yet. One team member stopped to tell the visitors how he had spent eleven days of a very busy work schedule watching, recording, and following the movement of materials through the plant to understand how the process could be improved. Another team member had enlisted in a computer course in order to help support the program, and two team leaders had begun college courses to build upon their skills.

Finishing their cups of coffee, the academic team was greeted by Kevin Hall, the works manager, who had organized a plant tour to show the improvements made since their last visit. As in the previous tour, Hall started at the point where trucks arrived to off-load bottles and bulk containers of base oils. If something seemed to be missing, it was. Where had all the inventory gone? As the tour progressed, the lack of inventory made the plant look large and light and the footsteps of the team echoed loudly.

The frantic activity had also subsided. Workers had managed to lift both productivity and quality at a more relaxed pace. As each team leader took over his or her part of the tour, the atmosphere was charged with positive statements and a list of successes achieved in a period of days. After the tour, Dempster asked for comments about the new plant, but once again he refused to take the praise that the facility deserved and dismissed comments by saying, "We have only just begun."

In the case of the lubricants teams, problems were tackled one at a time and were solved once identified. For instance, on the filling lines where plastic bottles were filled with blended lubricant and labeled, minutes were saved by reducing the downtime and adjustments made by line operators during the process of changeovers. When the savings in minutes are multiplied by the number of changes in a day and then the number of times the lines are changed in a year, these minutes reflect a very good return to the bottom line. Therefore, creating a management system that focused direction but left the velocity of change to the people who knew the most about the process allowed a much faster introduction of improvement. Indeed, during the initial phase of the management system, change was the only common denominator in the facility. Nothing stood still as teams moved quickly to "debottleneck" an area and then follow the product to the next area for attention.

❖ Creating a management system that focused direction but left the velocity of change to the people who knew the most about the process allowed a much faster introduction of improvement.

Once change began to gather momentum, the next stage was to maintain a record of the facility for posterity. In the drive for world class, being able to benchmark the position from where the organization started is an important step often forgotten. A video camera was used both for capturing the new-looking facility and also to videotape the activities as they occurred. The filling team was one of the first to grasp the new tool, and it was not long before every changeover was being analyzed by the team in front of a television in the boardroom as groups of operators, maintainers, and logisticians pored over individual video frames to see whether the process could be improved. The exercise proved a valuable social tool; teams began to act cross-functionally, had fun, and injected Yorkshire humor into the improvement effort.

On a more serious note, the lessons learned by the collective teams were interesting. Without bias or opinion, people could see their contributions to the whole system and, more important, the

145

consequences of their actions for other teams in the business. The result was the cementing of the three-tier system. Planners, maintainers, and operators could help each other to achieve much greater levels of change and efficiency than could the individual teams.

❖ People could see their contributions to the whole system and, more important, the consequences of their actions for other teams in the business.

It may seem odd that a small company should be so preoccupied with minutes, but to the Q8 lubricant plant in Leeds every minute counted regardless of whether the time was spent in planning production, receiving materials, blending, filing, or maintaining the plant. Time is also a common unit of measure between individuals and the group, and between groups in the three-tier system. It has also proved a powerful tool for showing which actions provide low or negative contribution to the company—actions that may have been taken for many years in the belief that they were assisting the production process and creating efficiency. When analyzed by teams across the entire company, the same actions become exposed in the light of optimizing the flow of material in a holistic manner. The real importance of any individual action can then be measured.

By providing an analysis tool that benchmarks the current position of the company activity, the team could calculate the rate of change and associated decay curves with any project. To highlight the work undertaken to address minutes in the changeover, to reduce the changeover time from sixty minutes to ten minutes in one step is an improvement of 600 percent, or a step change of a factor of six. However, to radically transform the organization in such a manner can cause trauma and a short-term loss of production; using the half-life approach, the team could manage the reduction in changeover times by halving each target. From the baseline of sixty minutes, the first stage was to reduce the time by 50 percent to 30 percent over a time horizon of a couple of days. Achieving this result allowed the targeting of the next stage to go from thirty to fifteen minutes in a week and from fifteen to seven minutes in a further two-week period.

It became evident during a meeting with the plant teams that the rapid progress had been achieved without needing to invest anything other than small amounts of money. What had been achieved would not rank as a scientific breakthrough; rather teams of key fact-holders had worked together to solve common problems. The progress had been driven by the teams' apportioning responsibility for certain aspects of the order fulfillment process.

THE THREE-TIER SYSTEM AND TEAMS IN ACTION

The changeover group is a good example of the power of the three-tier system and fundamental business improvements. Once focused, the group began to generate ideas quickly, and decisions were almost instantaneous. One of the major problems with any changeover is ensuring that the new product is taken into the machine in the most optimal way. For example, the new bottle is guided to the filling head in the most appropriate manner. To solve this problem, the team agreed to color-code the guide rails of the conveyor system so that different bottle sizes would be given a set of predetermined colors, eliminating the minutes needed to adjust the machine. To save even more time, the locking mechanisms of the guide rails were changed so that nuts and bolts were replaced with simple turn bolts, further eliminating the time taken to correctly set the line. Having problem-solved the in-feed to the filling heads, the attention of the team was turned to the filling heads themselves.

By a process of analysis and recording, it was discovered that time could be saved by ensuring that the filling heads could be adjusted quickly. However, the complexity of the machine meant that a different set of solutions was needed. In this instance, the team decided to standardize the fixtures on the machine and dedicate changeover tools to the actual machine. To achieve this, a tool holder was placed on the machine, and all tools were positioned so that they could be reached easily and used effectively. This simple solution meant that an operator would know immediately if all the tools were ready for the coming changeover and that the tool he or she required was being used during the changeover if it was not in its permanent position. The result of this activity was the reduction in the time needed to change the production lines between products.

The changeover time–reduction team was not the only team in the facility; parallel groups had been established. One such group was developed to identify waste of materials in the factory and to ensure that every item of materials was used to the utmost effect. In lubricant blending and packaging, the assumption is that there will inevitably be a certain amount of wasted packaging as a result of the process itself. Therefore, it was customary for some items such as bottles, caps, labels, and boxes to be discarded for one reason or another. This was not acceptable to the Leeds plant, and, with a degree of rivalry, the materials-handling personnel led the charge to reduce this area of visible waste. After a few days the result of their efforts was a 40 percent reduction in waste, an accompanied reduction of 30 percent in the floor space required for packaging materials, and a reduction of 60 percent in the pallets needed to support production at the plant.

A third team also joined the action network of improvement and decided to address the reduction in time needed to bring supplied products and base oils into the production site. This team started by investigating how products were purchased, and then, awaiting the next truck's arrival at the factory gate, followed each and every activity through to the dispatch of the finished product to the third-party logistician. On the arrival of a truck containing oil additives, they hurriedly followed the driver and truck throughout the facility, at each stage noting what happened to the product until the materials handlers collected the product and placed it safely away. Problem solving as a group, the team decided to create an entirely new way of handling the traffic to the site. The yard was painted to form marshaling lines for the inbound trucks, all paperwork was standardized, and trucks were handled in sequence and off-loaded or loaded in the shortest time possible. As a result, vehicles were turned around quickly, and the traditional high fluctuations in vehicle arrivals was flattened to a nice, steady pace. The overall result of this activity was a decrease of some 30 percent in the time required to conduct the receiving activities.

This tidal wave of reform and the positive enthusiasm displayed by everyone at the plant is exemplary, leading to a fundamental lesson for all companies: Gain control over what you do first—before you spend any money on making the next big investment.

❖ Gain control over what you do first—before you spend any money on making the next big investment.

As a result of these team activities, many of the actions in the short-term plan were achieved quickly and allowed the company to begin focusing on the medium-term issues that affect the factory and the need for higher levels of management intervention and change in the system. The success in both the short- and medium-term campaigns can be seen to originate from three areas: the leadership style of the management team, the response of employees once they were challenged to meet new performance targets, and the ability of the company to make radical improvements without incurring huge financial burdens. A by-product of this approach was a new feeling of pride that grew as each area in the factory transformed to release its strengths and capabilities within the company context rather than simply to be hemmed in as a narrowly prescribed function within the business.

A notable side effect of this work has been a rise in the number of visitors to the plant and the amount of coffee consumed on a daily basis. Visitors from all over the Q8 lubricant and petroleum divisions have been escorted around the site. Although the carpet in the reception area shows signs of the numbers of visitors the company receives, the enthusiasm for becoming world class has not subsided but has grown. Even though the company maintains its number one position, it continues to strive for the vision of the perfect factory, in which no minute is lost in supplying lubricants to the customer.

SMALL FACILITY, MIGHTY VISION

The Q8 case highlights a company that, by virtue of its small size, could not develop an all-embracing three-tier system but adapted the approach to create a management system that draws from the same organizational and operational characteristics as those displayed by much larger organizations.

The senior team acted (as at Trico Australia) as a think tank and a focusing vehicle. It also played the role of the expert resource provider and target setter because, said Dempster, "I just don't have the management layers to create more than two tiers of teams, and any more would be wasteful." Thus, under the senior team Dempster created a series of area-related action teams as well as a control structure that assigned duties to functional areas within the business. The advantage of this structure was that it was quick to set up, very flexible, and could provide for very rapid communication and employee empowerment. Improvement activity could be delegated to personnel who understood the impact of tiny improvements within a much larger supply chain.

❖ Improvement activity could be delegated to personnel who understood the impact of tiny improvements within a much larger supply chain.

It would be wrong to underestimate the strength of the three-tier approach to management at the site and the new teamwork structure at Q8. The new approach provided many new sources of competitive advantage for the company in terms of faster communication and laid the cornerstone for a truly world-class company. This was not achieved by spending hours deliberating the strategic plan, but by quickly communicating the need to change far and wide within the organization and by managing change in the day-to-day business operations, which are often far removed from strategic documents of what should be happening within an organization. The focus on managing order fulfillment combined with the new system of process management has been the key to the development, profitability, and enthusiasm generated in the plant.

Shared by all of the examples in this chapter has been improved control of the order fulfillment process, a core process that retains satisfied customers and allows all areas of the business to participate in the new working system. Each case shown has implemented a version of the three-tier system of management, adapted for each company's unique markets and environment. What stands out is the building of a coherent framework for both radical *and* continuous improvements to happen simultaneously, a buy-in from the people directly and indirectly involved, and a platform from which to increase high performance of the order fulfillment process. The end result is to more fully exploit the strategic expectation of the organization for customer satisfaction.

NOTES

1. This information is drawn directly from Amrik Sohal, "Developing a Lean Production Organization: An Australian Case Study," *International Journal of Operations & Production Management,* vol. 16, no. 2, 1996, pp. 91–102.
2. More on JUKI can be found in Takeo Okayama, "Delivery Control at JUKI Corporation: An Example of Cross-Functional Management Improvement," in Kenji Kurogane (ed.), *Cross-Functional Management: Principles and Practical Applications* (Tokyo: Asian Productivity Organization, 1993). First published in Japanese in 1988.
3. The *value stream* is a term coined by James Womack and Daniel Jones in their article "From Lean Production to the Lean Enterprise" (*Harvard Business Review,* March–April, 1994). The value stream mapping tools used at Q8 include process activity mapping, supply chain response matrix, demand amplification mapping, production variety funnel, and decision point analysis. These were used with four products reflecting different market channels, pack size, product characteristics, and manufacturing paths.

PART IV

External Partners

Chapter 12

SUPPLIERS ON THE TEAM

Nowhere in business is there greater potential for benefiting from . . . interdependency than between customer firms and their suppliers. This is the largest remaining frontier for gaining competitive advantage—and nowhere has such a frontier been more neglected.

Peter Drucker, *The Changing World of the Executive* (London: Heinemann, 1982).

We often forget that for all the seemingly fantastic communication tools we have, it is the informal exchanges of information that often produce the most beneficial results.

Lance Dixon, Director of Purchasing and Logistics, Bose Corporation

A young British operations manager was in discussion with his CEO about working closely with suppliers. The CEO, a former Big Three automotive buyer, looked at his junior kindly and recalled, "In my day, you gained promotion by the number of suppliers you could put out of business." "But," he was ready to acknowledge, "maybe things have changed." The operations manager hoped so as he was keenly aware of the detrimental effect a poorly managed supplier base would have on any future growth and profitability of his company.

Taking the matter in hand, he decided to take a closer look at the manufacturing process for which he was responsible. A quick calculation showed that, at best, he had good control of only 30 percent of the process. An estimated further 30 percent of the process belonged to his key suppliers, whom he had visited occasionally, more as an industrial tourist than as an expert observer. But worst of all was the remaining 40 percent of indirect suppliers whose processes he had never seen and over which he had no direct leverage. He had never met these people, never coordinated any of their activities with his, let alone sought any improvements. There had to be a better way, he was sure.

Some time later the same manager was discussing with a senior Japanese manager his idea about bringing some key direct and indirect suppliers together on a regular basis for strategic and operational improvements. After listening carefully to the explanation, the Japanese manager displayed no surprise at such an approach given the long Japanese history of intimate supplier involvement. When the young operations manager stated that this strategy was almost unique in the United Kingdom, the Japanese manager was astonished this time and asked how British companies could possibly compete in world markets without such cooperation. The answer: They couldn't. But the British manager thought that best left unsaid.

Some time later the operations manager attended a symposium on purchasing and supply chain management. He was quickly disillusioned. Although speaker after speaker talked about supplier partnerships and strategic procurement, the overriding message was narrowly focused on the role of the purchasing *function*. In the closing session there was a heated debate about why no CEOs were attending the event and why companies were not taking purchasing seriously.

The operations manager was at a loss until he encountered an academic who looked at the issue through a very different lens. First, the professor explained, purchasing people think of themselves as "strategic," but although they may create "strategic plans," these are all too often unrelated to general company strategy or marketplace requirements. Second, he explained, they attempt to integrate with suppliers without other functional support from within their companies. Third, they talk about partnership and close relationships but don't really have a process to plan by, a road map to follow, or a set of strategic standards to gauge their progress. "Apart from that," he noted with wry humor, "they seem to be doing a pretty good job!"

❖ Purchasing people think of themselves as "strategic," but although they may create "strategic plans," these are all too often unrelated to general company strategy or marketplace requirements.

From these insights the operations manager saw right away what was needed: a cross-organizational supplier integration process driven by corporate strategy and controlled by a few key metrics, or benchmarks. In short, the company needed a process that took the needs of the whole business into account.

He kept wondering what it was, though, that Japanese manufacturers had learned when it came to integrating suppliers into their businesses.

SUPPLIER INTEGRATION

An attempt to interpret Japan's evident success, particularly in discrete manufacturing (that is, component assembly, as in the automotive, electronics, and camera industries), suggests four primary explanations. The first is a coherent, holistic strategy and a method of deploying it throughout a network of interlinked organizations. The second is a standardized manufacturing approach typified by the vaunted Toyota Production System (TPS). Third, most large Japanese manufacturing companies have a set of complementary cross-organizational processes. Fourth, and until recently ignored by the majority of Western companies, is a coherent *supplier integration* process, explained in detail in this chapter. The dynamic interrelationship of these attributes helps explain the underlying managerial mechanisms of Japanese postwar manufacturing successes. As the economic analyst Robert Samuelson reported, however, not every company in Japan can claim world-class status. "About 40 percent of their manufacturing sector is truly world class, but much of the rest is truly dreadful," he noted. "In food processing, capital productivity is about 64 percent the U.S. level. And outside of manufacturing, about 70 percent of the economy, is worse."[1]

There are, however, important lessons to be learned from Japan's best. As one senior executive from Kirin Brewery stressed, one should "manage the supply chain for competitive advantage and not [just] to reduce costs." Indeed, the Japanese success suggests that draconian and narrowly focused cost-cutting programs of the sort advocated by some executives are potentially counterproductive. A close interweaving of supplier activities can bring a far more systemic approach to cost reduction, quality assurance, and delivery improvement in processes such as order fulfillment and new product development.

Since the late 1980s, this challenge has been taken up by leading Western companies in a variety of industries in North America and Europe. Robert J. Eaton, chairman of Chrysler Corporation has commented that "effective relations with all tiers of our suppliers represent one of Chrysler's greatest opportunities to add value to our vehicles." In Europe, Ian Robertson, managing director of Land Rover, echoed the same ambitions by charting "the goal of fewer closer, more capable suppliers . . . [as] the fundamental building block of everything that Rover is trying to achieve, and the reason it is the top priority within its quality strategy."

❖ "[One should] manage the supply chain for competitive advantage and not just to reduce costs." Indeed, the Japanese success suggests that draconian and narrowly focused cost-cutting programs . . . are potentially counterproductive.

The issue when it comes to supplier integration is perhaps not whether it is of use but how to practically apply it. In that regard, a number of different approaches can be used:

- Supplier associations
- On-site suppliers
- Cross-exchanges of staff
- One-on-one working groups
- Supplier schools.

Although each of these has enormous merit and proven benefits, the supplier association is best at integrating suppliers and buyers into a seamless whole.

PREPARING FOR A SEAMLESS SUPPLY CHAIN

RS Components is part of Electro-Components, PLC, one of Europe's leading distributors of electronic, electrical, and mechanical components and instruments. The company sells its 70,000 products primarily through a state-of-the-art direct distribution system as well as a network of regional trade counters. It dispatches more than 15,000 orders per day from one million square feet of warehouse space and employs more than 3,000 staff in the United Kingdom, France, Germany, Italy, Austria, Denmark, Ireland, and Spain.

RS Components is structured around a well-knit "three tier" (senior management team, process teams, and action teams) culture that encourages cross-functional involvement as well as a very high level of customer service. This is borne out in the use of value stream groups to control the internal and external logistics processes, a style of management that allows the elimination of separate purchasing, inventory control, and marketing departments.[2] In their place, cross-organizational teams manage along product areas or value streams. Seventeen product areas are supported by very small dedicated competency centers in purchasing and inventory control.

RS Components is regarded by many within its industry as the "best of the best." The staff have a strong continual improvement motivation and an openness to learn and try out new ideas. It was no surprise, therefore, that in 1995 they saw value in joining a cross-industry research and networking forum called the Supply Chain Development Program (SCDP), which is facilitated by the Lean Enterprise Research Centre at Cardiff Business School and the Centre for Research in Strategic Purchasing and Supply at the University of Bath.[3]

The starting point for what turned into a supplier integration program at RS Components was a strategic review of the organization carried out by a cross-functional group in the company including the supply chain director, Keith Pacey. Two of this book's authors (Hines and Rich) acted as facilitators in this process. The review included the use of value stream mapping tools designed to highlight areas of opportunity and further development within companies. Although drawn from a variety of functional domains such as logistics, engineering, and industrial dynamics, the tools can be applied by cross-organizational teams both within and between organizations. In the case of RS Components, the tools were used primarily by the company and its direct suppliers.

The reason for the strategic review was not that the company was in trouble. Quite the reverse; it was easily outperforming its rivals. However, Keith Pacey and his staff realized that although the company might have been world-class in its distribution performance, other parts of the business needed improvement, such as the level of inventory held and lead times from suppliers, which averaged ten weeks. The value stream mapping was performed over a one-month period in late 1995, with these key findings:

- Internal value adding was low.
- There were many delay points in the flow of goods inward.
- The product quality was excellent.
- High urgency and complexity of the internal value stream was not reflected in the external value stream.
- Long supplier lead times were problematic because of relatively short internal lead times.
- Very high levels of available stock were common.
- There was lack of "pull" from market-based needs.
- Lack of integration with overseas branches was in evidence.
- Dislocations were occurring between purchasing and customer demand.

- Need for improved supplier on-time performance was necessary.
- There was a need to link customer "pull" with supplier demand.

The carefully executed mapping work did several things for RS Components. First, although it confirmed a number of hunches that staff had, it also gave the lie to a number of other gut feelings. Second, it created a shared understanding of what the real situation was, allowing the opportunity to manage according to real evidence, not theory. Third, it created a new and crucial desire by senior management to create a supplier integration program.

Work on the supplier integration program began in early 1996 and incorporated a three-tier system of management and a cascading series of teams, as shown in Figure 12.1.

The cascading system was put in place with as many members of the original mapping team as possible. For instance, Keith Pacey was brought in to the steering group, made up of senior managers and directors of the company from all the relevant functions involved. The purpose of the steering group, led by the head of the purchasing competency center, David Noble, was to ensure that a critical target was set for the program. This target was simply an unambiguously set at a doubling of stock turns within a three-year horizon. In addition this group scheduled a series of bimonthly meetings to measure the progress of the work, to ensure that adequate resources were being employed, and to make sure that nothing interrupted or disrupted the supplier integration process. The steering group made no attempt to tell the process facilitation or project teams how to achieve the outline target that had been set but provided the support to help them.

❖ The steering group made no attempt to tell the process facilitation or project teams how to achieve the outline target that had been set but provided the support to help them.

12.1. RS Component's three-tier system of management for supplier integration.

Group or Team	Role and Responsibilities
Steering Group (Tier 1: senior team)	• Set outline targets • Review progress of program • Ensure resource availability • Unblock functional barriers
Process Facilitation Team (Tier 2: process team)	• Learn and disseminate supplier integration process • Facilitate supplier integration process across project teams • Develop generic, motivational metrics • Measure performance of groups • Provide technical resources to project teams
Project Teams (Tier 3: action team)	• Implement supplier integration program with key suppliers • Monitor day-to-day development of supplier integration

The process facilitation team, led by Ian Kellie of the purchasing competency center, was formed from middle managers from the various key competency centers in the business. These included representatives from the central inventory support group, the strategic purchasing group, and two of the business team managers responsible for a number of product group teams. This process facilitation was also supported by Hines and Rich. A key responsibility was to develop a set of metrics and performance gaps to motivate and guide action teams in planning and executing their day-to-day work. These are shown in Figure 12.2. Around these goals the team designed the broad guidelines of an optimal supplier integration process and facilitated its dissemination to the individual project or action teams. It also established ties between different project teams and ensured that knowledge was shared between them.

12.2. RS Components: Motivational metrics and performance gaps developed by process facilitation team.

Metric	Target Performance	Current Performance	Gap
Average lead time	5 weeks	8.23 weeks	3.23
Average stock turns	6	3.6	2.4
Forecast accuracy	45%	38.2%	6.8%
Forecast variability ratio	1:2	1:3.1	—
Delivery on time	95%	74%	21%
Delivery correct quantity	95%	62%	33%
Rejections	1,000 ppm	5,314 ppm	4,314
Customer returns	10,000 ppm	60,815 ppm	50,815

These few key metrics do not seek simply to measure or audit the performance of the suppliers but to gauge the degree of supplier integration. Some of them, like forecast variability, are more a measure of RS Components's performance. Others, such as delivery on time, are more a reflection of the suppliers' performance. A third group, including average stock turn at RS Components, are a reflection of how effectively the downstream customers and upstream suppliers work together.

Individual action teams are made accountable for attaining these targets a step at a time. Meantime, the process-owning team provides technical resources and support when required. The first action team was created in early 1996, with members representing the value stream: a buyer, an inventory controller, and a product (marketing) manager. They are supported by staff members from quality assurance, goods inward, and accounting. The team is led by a champion, who in this case happens to be the buyer.

The role of this team is to implement the supplier integration process with key suppliers. Of the thirty-two suppliers in this product area, seven were chosen on the basis of the expenditures for their products as well as potential and previous proactive stance toward RS Components. These seven represented around half of the external expenditures by the product group and were targeted for an annualized 25 percent increase in business in 1996. The companies are a mixture of European manufacturers and distributors of non-European products. At the start of the process they had a wide span of abilities and divergent attitudes toward supplier integration.

CREATING A SUPPLIER ASSOCIATION

The operating mechanism or framework chosen for the supplier integration process was the Supplier Association. A supplier association is a mutually benefiting group of a company's most important suppliers brought together on a regular basis to coordinate, cooperate, and share best practice. The development of such groups, pioneered in Europe by one of the authors of this book, is now providing competitive advantage to more than four hundred companies.[4] His methods were used by RS Components to

- Raise awareness by the customer and key suppliers of the need to change and what to do
- Educate the different companies on how to make the change
- Serve as a vehicle for successful implementation

❖ A supplier association is a mutually benefiting group of a company's most important suppliers brought together on a regular basis to coordinate, cooperate, and share best practice.

As mentioned, seven companies were invited by the project team to join the RS Components's supplier association, which held its first meeting in February 1996 at a local hotel. Prior to this, the team had undertaken a careful analysis of what they wanted to get out of the supplier association and how this might be achieved. Value stream analysis tools (VALSATs)[5] were used to brainstorm about the outputs that RS Components wanted from the program, with importance weightings developed for each. Members of the project team deliberated different approaches to achieve the desired outputs. They developed a correlation of the improvements required and possible methods to use, with a range of scores given depending on the closeness of correlation. They determined the total usefulness for each method by multiplying its weighting by the correlation score and summing the result by columns.

The result was a ranking of the top ten supplier integration methods to achieve the needs of customers. This was presented to the supplier association members at the first meeting together with a briefing on the goals of the supplier association and how it could be used in the supplier integration program. During this event, and in more detail afterward, individual suppliers were asked to undertake a similar VALSAT exercise on what they wanted to achieve from the program. This allowed the company to take their views into account before deciding what work to undertake. The results of these two exercises, shown as follows, isolated ten key methods.

Rank	RS Components's Suggested Improvement Methods	Suppliers' Suggested Improvement Methods
1	Self-certification	Comanaged inventory
2	Due-date performance	Due-date performance
3	Vendor rating	Milk rounds (delivery)
4	Stabilize schedules	Ship to stock
5	Milk rounds (delivery)	Stabilize schedules
6	Comanaged inventory	Standard packs
7	EDI (Electronic Data Interchange)	Standard product information
8	Replenishment modules	Replenishment modules
9	Hotline to suppliers	EDI
10	Safety stock at suppliers'	Self-certification

Although RS Components and the suppliers clearly had different requirements, there was a very close alignment of improvement methods. Seven methods were common to both top ten lists. However, only six of these were feasible in the short/medium time horizon. Some would require joint work and some input from the customer or supplier alone.

Top-Rated Joint Improvement Methods and Inputs Required

1	Comanaged inventory	Mostly supplier initiative
2	Due-date performance	Mostly supplier; better information from RS Components needed
3	Milk round	Mostly supplier; RS Components to coordinate
4	Self-certification	Shared work
5	Stabilize schedules	RS Components initiative
6	EDI (Electronic Data Interchange)	Shared work

The awareness-raising stage complete, it was then necessary to educate and share knowledge about how to effect these improvements and craft an action plan to meet the improvement targets. The company undertook this with a series of workshops in early 1996. Participants drew up detailed plans permitting both RS Components and the key suppliers to implement the improvements either together or, in a focused way, on their own, depending on the particular circumstances.

After the early success of this work, RS Components launched a second project team working in the connectors product area with a similar-size group of suppliers. This work is facilitated by the same process facilitation team. Over time such project teams will be used within the supplier association mechanism to integrate key suppliers with each of the product group areas.

SUPPLIER INTEGRATION IN THE AUTOMOTIVE INDUSTRY

Rigorous supplier integration is widely prevalent in the automotive industry because the industry has a high buy-in content and operates under severe competitive cost and quality pressure. Some of the leaders in this work have been Toyota in Japan, Rover in the United Kingdom, Honda in the United States, and Hyundai in Korea. Each of these companies operates a supplier association, either in name or action.[6] For Toyota the supplier integration initiative, already more than thirty years old, is a strategic effort deemed critical to the competitive strength of the company.

How Toyota Saved $1.5 Billion in 1994

We have been cutting costs continually for more than half a century. But the Japanese recession and the strong yen have forced us to pursue dramatic new cost savings. Continual small improvements remain important—they add up. But we have also needed to make some really big changes. . . . (One of the) six ways we have done that . . . (is to) encourage lean production practices at our suppliers and at their suppliers. . . .

The price of a new car reflects the cost of all the components that go into the car and the cost of all the parts and materials that go into those components. Our price competitiveness has benefited as our suppliers have used the Toyota Production System to achieve continuing gains in efficiency. And our competitiveness will increase further as our suppliers' suppliers and their suppliers adopt elements of that system to raise their efficiency.

"A sense of crisis, a hands-on commitment by top management, and the participation of employees"—That's what it takes for most suppliers to get serious about the Toyota Production System, according to Tomoyuki Torii. . . . He speaks from experience. Torii is a productivity engineer at Aisin Seiki Co., Ltd., a large manufacturer that supplies a diversity of automotive parts to Toyota and to other automakers. He has devoted much of his career to working with Aisin suppliers who request assistance in raising efficiency and quality.

One of Torii's success stories is Hisada Kogyosho Co., Ltd., a metal-working company that supplies door-frame parts and other items to Aisin. That company, which employs about 350 people, has achieved dramatic gains in efficiency over the past two years. Labor productivity is up more than 40 percent. And inventories are down 50 percent.

"We had dallied with the Toyota Production System occasionally," explains Hisada's founder and president Yoshimitsu Hisada" . . . But we didn't stick with it. Business was good. We might not have been as efficient as we could have been. But we were able to turn a profit and keep our people employed without subjecting ourselves to the rigors of lean production. Then came the slump. That lit a fire under us. Everyone in the company saw that we needed to get lean or perish. That's when we called on the people at Aisin and worked with them to put our plants on a leaner footing. Things are going to stay tough until the Japanese economy picks up. But I shudder to think where we would be today if we hadn't made our move when we did."[7]

As part of its supplier integration and support process, Toyota in Japan offers an unrivaled program of activities, including:

- Top management group meetings
- Quality awards

- Technology development support
- One-to-one assistance
- Quality assurance audits
- Automation workshops
- Logistics workshops
- Toyota production workshops
- Supplier association activities

The supplier association activities are far from a stand-alone outpost of activity. Toyota and its direct suppliers interact through four different supplier associations, which the suppliers are free to join as they wish. A total of 250—virtually all of their key suppliers—find value in doing so. Three of these groups are for parts makers in different regions of Japan. The other is for facility providers. The largest supplier association, the Tokai Kyohokai, acts as a three-tier system of management in itself. The responsibilities and frequency of formal interactions there are summarized in the following table:

Senior Team

Meetings	
Board/Assembly	7 per year

Process Teams

Management Meetings	
General Affairs Committee	8 per year
Other Management	3 per year
Process Meetings	
Quality Committee	8 per year
Cost Committee	9 per year
Safety & Health Committee	7 per year
Divisional Meetings	
Castings/Stampings	12 per year
Functional Parts	12 per year
Internal/External Parts	12 per year

Action Teams

Process Meetings	
Quality Committee	100 approx. per year
Cost Committee	100 approx. per year
Safety and Health Committee	50 approx. per year
Divisional Meetings	
Castings/Stampings	60 approx. per year
Functional Parts	60 approx. per year
Internal/External Parts	60 approx. per year

Toyota's high dependence on meetings as an integrating mechanism, a measure that might seem counterproductive to efficient work, ensures direct person-to-person contact as well as an open channel of communication both at work and in later social encounters. At the senior team level the supplier association board of management meets every two months. It is made up of the presidents of major suppliers and often invites key management from Toyota to attend. This highest-level team sets policies, steers the direction, and discusses target areas for the supplier community. This information is then used to direct the activities of the various process teams.

Three types of process teams are proposed. The first, involving all of the suppliers, is used to disseminate information from the senior team, which involves information exchange and discussions of how outline targets might be achieved. The second type of process team is concerned with those cross-organizational processes that are important to the success of each member of the supplier association. Although there is some variability from year to year, cost and quality teams are employed every year. In 1994, there was a safety and health team.

The purpose of the second type of process team is to identify how the respective cross-organizational processes can be coordinated between the individual suppliers and Toyota. In addition these groups seek ways to improve similar processes within their own companies by setting up cross-company action teams. The divisional process team undertakes a similar role, and its meetings are frequented by companies making the respective type of product. In the same way the divisional process team directs action teams for specific implementation programs.

The action teams are not simply one team meeting up to 100 times per year; rather, as in the case of the cost committee action team, they are a series of splinter groups that actually implement improvements. Each splinter group typically contains about six companies, one of which may be Toyota. The splinter teams meet perhaps once a month to implement a specific improvement in one or more companies. Their success is judged against specific motivational or dynamic targets set by either the process team or the individual action team. In this way Toyota externalizes the three-tier system of management to include key members of its extensive supplier community.

SUPPLIER INTEGRATION IN OTHER INDUSTRIES

Another approach to supplier integration is use of co-located supplier teams. In the United States, a reputed one thousand or more companies now practice variations of the widely propagated just-in-time program JIT II™, invented by the Bose Corporation, the Massachusetts maker of industrial and consumer sound systems.[8] Use of guest engineers and third-party logisticians inside customers' premises is an established habit in Japan and some parts of Europe.[9] Indeed, in Japan this method of supplier integration is rather more complex, involving transfer of staff from customer to supplier and vice versa. A system with a particularly novel name called the Descent from Heaven is used. Older employees who may be regarded as superfluous are given the opportunity of moving to suppliers through the process of *ami-kudari* ("descent from heaven"). These employees are placed in affiliated companies as sources of knowledge about customers for which they formerly worked.

❖ Older employees who may be regarded as superfluous are given the opportunity of moving to suppliers through the process of *ami-kudari* ("descent from heaven").

In Bose's case, under the leadership of Lance Dixon, the director of purchasing and logistics, the company set out in the late 1980s to gain a higher degree of supplier integration by inviting a few key vendors to relocate one or more staff members to the main engineering site. These nine vendor personnel now account for 35 percent of Bose's purchases. Said Dixon, "We basically got rid of the salesman and the purchasing officer. The supplier is empowered to place orders by accessing our central data sources of inventory. In effect we give him or her a blank purchase order for them to sign and issue."[10] Although this kind of blind trust might quicken the heart rate of old-line accountants, the system turns out to be surprisingly self-policing. "At first there was a visceral feeling that someone would get their hands in the till and disappear to a resort beach in the Caribbean. "But," said Dixon, "while the risk may be there they only get to cheat once. And if they do they've lost their relationship with us forever. In fact the supplier will leap to make the buyer happy."

At Bose the purchased commodities include high-volume requirements involving plastic tooling and parts, metal parts, corrugated packaging, printing, importing procedures, and domestic and international transportation. The key element is that the vendor's staff are not only physically located inside but are empowered by the Bose customer's purchasing function as the link between Bose's planning department and the vendor's production plant. "In fact this is akin to giving me a staff of nine people to work with whom I never would have had authorized on a budget ever before," said Dixon. "What we don't do is bet the house on an external partner coming up with a key technology," emphasized Dixon, acknowledging that "other firms have gone that far."

A DAILY INSIGHT INTO JIT II, AT BOSE CORPORATION

To illustrate better how all this works, let's follow Chris LaBonte, In-Plant Representative from G&F Industries around for a typical day at Bose.

G&F Industries supplies plastic injection molding tooling, plastic parts, and metal parts to Bose, shipping to various Bose plants worldwide, or utilizing the G&F Ireland facility.

Chris starts some days at his plant in Sturbridge, Massachusetts, where he controls various production schedules with a status review of Bose in-process parts.

He arrives at the Bose Westboro manufacturing plant, where he confers with John Argitis, Jr., the other G&F In-Plant Representative. John is heavily involved in the daily planning and ordering of G&F material for this particular Bose plant, using Bose purchase orders from his location in the plant purchasing department. (G&F is one of the two companies that have asked to place two persons to keep up with all aspects of the business.)

Chris arrives at his office in the corporate purchasing department late morning, where he confers with the Bose Framingham plant material planners and receives related material requisitions. He "calls them in" to his plant after sign-off by the Bose purchasing manager on orders that exceed his dollar authorization per order, the same as any Bose buyer. At one o'clock, he attends a Bose New Product Project review at the Bose mountain headquarters location, gathering information of any importance on parts G&F will be supplying.

Two o'clock brings Chris into contact with Bose design engineers who have questions on process possibilities and cost trade-offs on a plastic part and various materials. At three, a quality control issue is addressed with corporate & plant quality personnel.

Today, Chris is leaving early for the airport to fly to the Bose San Luis, Mexico, facility, where a new product start-up is to take place with various G&F parts. Having participated in the pilot production in the Bose Westboro plant, he is well-versed in all aspects of the product start-up and possible difficulties."

"What it's all about really," summarized Dixon, "is better communication that leads to far better managed vendor inventory." Bose's program has been so successful and in demand from other companies that Sherwin Greenblatt, CEO, founded an education and research center to train other companies in JIT II.

SUPPLIER SCHOOLS

A small number of Western organizations have set about integrating with suppliers by educating the suppliers in manufacturing or management approaches schools or "universities." Among some of the first companies to do this were Ford, Motorola, Digital, and Unipart (United Kingdom).

Motorola is the epitome of a multinational corporation seeking perfection through total quality. This goal was originally driven by

President Galvin's 1981 directive to increase quality levels 100-fold by 1992 and so achieve the elusive 6-sigma quality level (99.99966 percent). As a result of this pursuit of excellence, Motorola, the largest U.S. semiconductor manufacturer, is the world's largest cellular phone maker, and generates sales of more than $1 billion in Japan's hard-to-generate domestic market. In 1988 Motorola's success was recognized in the award of the prestigious Malcolm Baldrige Award.

Motorola set up cross-organizational teams to search out best-in-class suppliers and then worked closely with those suppliers, particularly in the early design phases of new product development. The major goal was improved quality; indeed, all suppliers were asked to apply for the Malcolm Baldrige Award if they wanted to continue to supply Motorola. This approach was designed to speed implementation of the 6-sigma program by suppliers. This process was accompanied by setting up Motorola University in 1989, an institution primarily designed to train and educate Motorola's own workforce and managers. The university concentrated on the needs that Motorola had in creating a better workforce. As an institution, it is obviously helping the company to unlock the abilities of its employees, but it is doing far more. It is also doing the same for suppliers and even for Motorola's customers. William Wiggenhorn, vice president of training and education and president of Motorola U, explains, "Motorola University is presently open to the employees of our suppliers, of our principal customers."[12]

Behind all these efforts at companies like RS Components, Toyota, Bose, and Motorola is a well-understood effort to open up lines of communication both face-to-face and electronic. But more important is the implicit awareness of the dynamics of nonlinear interactions, those that occur unpredictably just because the principal actors are present around a table or a coffee machine. This, in fact, is where much of the payoff occurs.

NOTES
1. Robert J. Samuelson, "Is There a Savings Gap?" *Newsweek,* June 17, 1996, p. 56.

2. The value stream mapping tools used at RS Components include process activity mapping, supply chain response matrix, demand amplification mapping, quality filter mapping, and decision point analysis. These were used with a group of nine products within one product category area. A further and more detailed discussion of the value stream mapping tools can be found in Peter Hines and Nick Rich, "The Seven Value Stream Mapping Tools," *International Journal of Operations and Production Management,* vol. 17, no. 1, 1997.

3. The Supply Chain Development Program is a five-year action research program sponsored by eighteen of Europe's leading supply chain management companies. The firms are drawn from the food, retail, automotive, electronics, clothing, service, and process industries.

4. The supplier association method was pioneered in Europe by Peter Hines. In early 1996, twenty-eight European companies were using this method as part of their supplier integration work with, in total, approximately four hundred suppliers. Evidence from the first groups set up in the early 1990s suggests that the incremental improvement rate made by suppliers is around 36 percent faster than would have been the case had they not been involved in the work. In addition, supplier improvements are not only faster but also in the precise direction required by customers owing to the strategy-sharing nature of the supplier association. Further information on the supplier association can be found in Peter Hines, *Creating World Class Suppliers: Unlocking Mutual Competitive Advantage,* Pitman Publishing, London, 1994.

5. The value stream analysis tool is based on the quality function deployment (QFD) method employed in new product development. It allows for a rigorous analysis of what improvements are required in any value stream situation. It also allows different solutions to be tested for expected success and thus helps optimize the use of scarce resources in any inter- or intracompany improvement process. A fuller discussion of the tool can be found in Peter Hines, Nick Rich, and Malaika Hittmeyer, "Competing Against Ignorance: Advantage Through Knowledge," *International Journal of Physical Distribution and Logistics Management,* vol. 17, no. 1, 1997.

6. This list is far from inclusive but represents some of the leading automotive assemblers in different parts of the world using the method. Other assemblers using a similar approach include Toyota (United States, Canada), NUMMI (United States), Volvo (Belgium), Nissan (United Kingdom), Mercedes (Germany), Volkswagen (Germany), and virtually all of the Japanese car assemblers in Japan. Further information on Honda's supplier integration work can be found in Kevin R. Fitzgerald, "For Superb Supplier Development—Honda Wins!" *Purchasing Magazine,* September 21, 1995, pp. 32–40.

7. Excerpts taken from "Toyota Motor Corporation, How We Saved $1.5 Billion" (Annual Report) (Toyota City: Toyota Motor Corporation, 1994).

8. JIT II is a registered trademark of the Bose Corporation. More information

on JIT II can be found in Lance Dixon, "JIT II" *79th Annual International Purchasing Conference Proceedings,* 1994, pp. 185–190. For an excellent insight see "Bose Corporation: JIT II Program" case studies prepared by the Harvard Business School, Ref. N9-694-001 (March 8, 1994).

9. Further information on the Japanese use of staff transfer can be found in Peter Hines, *Creating World Class Suppliers: Unlocking Mutual Competitive Advantage,* Pitman Publishing, London, 1994, pp. 152–159.

10. Quotations taken from presentations to the the International Association for Product Development (IAPD), June 12, 1996, in Marlboro, Massachusetts.

11. This account is taken from Lance Dixon, "JIT II," *79th Annual International Purchasing Conference Proceedings,* 1994, p. 187.

12. William Wiggenhorn, "Motorola U: When Training Becomes an Education," *Harvard Business Review,* vol. 90, no. 4, July–August 1990, pp. 71–83.

Chapter 13

CRAFTING
THE
TRANSITION

An inflection point occurs where the old strategic picture dissolves and gives way to the new, allowing the business to ascend to new heights. However, if you don't navigate your way through an inflection point, you go through a peak and after the peak the business declines. It is around such inflection points that managers must puzzle and observe, "Things are different. Something has to change."

Andrew S. Grove, *Only the Paranoid Survive: How to Exploit the Crisis Points That Challenge Every Company and Career* (New York: Currency Doubleday, 1996).

Welsh companies are featured in this book for a reason. Although Wales is small geographically and counts a total population of only three million inhabitants, it has emerged as one of Europe's most dynamic subregions alongside the more acclaimed economic urban minimotors of Milan, Barcelona, Lyon, or Stuttgart. Various companies, many of them transplants to Wales from at least a dozen different countries, have tapped a vein of creative human talent willing to experiment and innovate technologically and organizationally. Although Mitel, described in Chapter 7, is an exceptional case fitted to an advanced technology, others are far more conventional manufacturing industries. Through them one can see a region move rapidly from an obsolete century-old industrial system of management to one that is attuned to the agility and leanness of a knowledge-driven global economy.

This is happening in Pontypool, South Wales, lying at the threshold of economic prosperity. Its grey legacy of coal and steel is giving way to an economic future based on fast-paced new companies such as the automotive component supplier Trico. In 1992, this manufacturer of car windshield wipers moved lock, stock, and barrel from a long-established London location to Pontypool. Part of the attraction was public subsidies allowing it to build a modern factory with world-class production facilities and methods. Another was a dedicated underemployed labor force willing to adapt to radically new ways of working. The move created, as a result, a rare opportunity to invent a new organizational culture and a far more collaborative family of suppliers. The latter is the subject of the story that follows.

A visitor's initial impressions of Trico are striking given the lingering legacy of sooty coal mines within living memory and eyesight. First to catch the eye is a collection of quality awards from world-class companies displayed in the reception area. It takes up a complete wall. Further one finds open-plan, uncluttered offices—still unusual in most of Europe—that exude calmness and efficiency. In numerous locations the company has mounted up-to-date notice boards displaying before and after Polaroid photographs of the surrounding work areas. And in a well-frequented corridor, everyone's pay scale by ranking is posted, from the managing director to the guard at the door. Immediately noticeable to an American visitor, for example, is the small gap between salaries of the highest and lowest ranked. Within the expansive shop floor, a sense of efficiency and order pervades. Notice boards abound with similar before and after photographs of respective work areas, stores, and toolroom areas. It is hard not to be impressed. This is a company working hard to make everyone feel a part of the whole.

❖ This is a company working hard to make everyone feel a part of the whole.

Three factors are responsible for what the visitor sees today. The first and perhaps most important was the move from London in 1992. This provided Trico with a one-time opportunity to scrap past habits and rethink both its internal processes and the way it dealt with its suppliers. The second was the joint launching of the Welsh Automotive Supplier Association by automaker Rover and the Welsh Development Agency's Source Wales team, led by Dennis Turner, which masterminded a series of innovative programs designed to create a new level of competitive ability within Welsh manufacturing companies. The third was their first meeting with Paul Morris, a Welsh consultant from a company called Supplier Association Partners, who was project managing the supplier association program for Source Wales.

It was late in 1993 when Trico, along with twenty-two of Rover's other strategic suppliers in Wales, was invited to a supplier association meeting by the carmaker, itself far along in a top-to-bottom redesign of its own operations influenced by its part-owner, Honda. At that time, the company's purchasing manager, Jim Taylor, and his boss, David Jones, were far from anticipating the radical implications this meeting would have for them and their company. In fact, they did not even know what a supplier association was. Instead, they were deeply skeptical of any new flavor-of-the-month initiative that their main customer, Rover, might be launching.

As it turned out, Rover was working hard to get past the rhetoric of partnership words and the reality of adversarial actions. These were exactly the kinds of contradictions that humorists such as Scott Adams and his cartoon character, Dilbert, thrive on. But now, its managers were attempting to move themselves and their supply chain into the next century as an extended world-class enterprise. As one of the Rover directors said in "executive-ese" at this first meeting, "We need to do more than just talk the talk, we need to walk the walk, we need to actually work together and implement real change." It made sense to Taylor and Jones, but were Rover and the Source Wales team actually going to deliver?

A few months later, Trico was invited to more events. Discussions took place, plans were drawn up, and both Trico and the other invited suppliers began to believe they could use shared know-how for mutual benefit. Significant improvements were made. Rover reported that members of the group had reduced quality failures by around 80 percent, while suppliers outside the Welsh Automotive Supplier Association had improved by only a few percentage points. Taylor and Jones could see that the process was working.

It was not long before Rover mentioned that their suppliers should start thinking about their own development. The Rover purchasing director commented, "We're not saying that you all need to rush away and set up your own supplier associations; that might not be the best vehicle, but we at Rover would be very interested in hearing about a better approach, because we haven't found one yet!"

This set Taylor and Jones thinking. Would the same collaborative process work for them and their suppliers? They attended a two-day briefing sponsored by Source Wales and run by consultant Paul Morris. After a day and a half they were still not convinced that a supplier association was the right thing for them. This could easily end up being all talk, they concluded. Then Morris opened a discussion on how two types of hard and soft benchmarking could be used to focus suppliers and allow for mutual target setting—akin to performance gaps. He also shared his experiences of problems encountered in setting up such groups and told those attending how to avoid the dreaded all-talk, no-action syndrome. Taylor and Jones constructed a new mental picture of what might be possible.

Morris showed the attendees a ten-stage checklist for a supplier association that, in his words, "ensured that there was not just a wish list for improvement, but a clearly defined process that would ensure that suppliers bought in, were aware of where they needed to improve, could become educated both in theory and practice, and could actually achieve change." This was what Taylor and Jones were waiting to hear. They took the ten-point check list and with Morris started to plan their own Trico campaign.

TRICO'S SUPPLIER ASSOCIATION

A name had to be agreed upon for the new supplier association. Morris happened to mention in passing that there was already a Trico Supplier Association in existence. Taylor and Jones were surprised, so Morris explained that much like the word *xerox* the name *trico,* linked to its own invention of the car windshield wiper, had become generic in Japan. There a trico simply meant a window wiper. Because of the widespread use of supplier associations in Japan, another wiper maker had called their group the Trico Supplier Association. Undaunted, Taylor suggested that the group needed a unique name anyway. After some discussion the name Trico Quest Supplier Association was chosen, with Quest being an acronym for quality and excellence through supplier teamwork. All that was required now was to develop an implementation strategy.

In an exercise in leadership and risk taking, Jones gave Taylor and Morris full authority to go ahead with his support for whatever they felt was the right approach. One condition was that whatever they did should be consistent with Trico's mission statement:

> It is the policy of Trico to provide products and services that give total customer satisfaction. Customers are those who buy our products, our suppliers, our staff, and all those with whom we have contact.

> We will treat each other with respect and strive for excellence in all we do to provide a high level of service to all customers—internal and external.

> We will maintain a culture based on continuous improvement in all we do and will train and fully involve every employee.

Like most mission statements it contained an ideal that was difficult to argue with but nearly impossible to achieve without a coherent process to help. Taylor and Morris set about creating one, at least for the supplier relationships. This could prove strategically important because half of Trico's cost of sales was based on products bought from its suppliers. Make an improvement there, they realized, and quality, cost, and delivery performance would be immediately affected. After several meetings in the autumn of 1994, a simple task scheduling Gantt chart was produced to guide the timing of this process.

The first step was to develop a strategy and implementation plan. Included were such questions as which suppliers to invite, how many meetings to have, what to focus on, and how to benchmark. Drawing on Morris's experience in helping to set up many other supplier associations, Taylor put together a strategy document. This twenty-one page document explained why the association was crucial to the achievement of the mission statement. It went on to define the Trico Quest Supplier Association as

> a mutually beneficial grouping of key suppliers linked together in a strategic alliance by their supply to Trico. A self-help team brought together on a regular basis to share knowledge and experience in an open and cooperative manner with the purpose of members mutually approving and developing skills, systems, and techniques, integrating processes, and eliminating wastes.

The document explained in greater detail why the association was being developed. It set both an ethical tone and a pragmatic one by describing the commitment Trico would make and that which its suppliers would honor (see Figure 13.1).

An implementation mechanism was drawn up in the strategy document that included the use of benchmarking, four management seminars per year with supplementary workshops run as required. All of this was designed to be within a framework of a shared-learning network. Last, the document outlined the types of mutual benefits to be sought. The benefits fell very much in line with the commitments being promised by Trico and its suppliers.

In January 1995, a group of nine suppliers were invited to a supplier invitation conference. These suppliers, although only about 10 percent of the total number, were responsible for a lion's share

13.1. Achieving Trico's mission statement: commitment to action.

The Commitment

Our operating practices are also receiving attention and we realize we have a role to play in supporting our suppliers; we are committed to:

* A better understanding of each other's needs
* Involve suppliers at the earliest stages of design
* Involve suppliers in internal project teams
* Encourage and promote timely and effective communication across all functions
* Listen and act upon criticism
* Strive continually to improve schedule stability
* Provide methods of measuring performance and improvement
* Provide benchmark positioning against best practice processes and practices
* Participate in and encourage joint continuous improvements
* Be open and honest
* Strive for quality and excellence in all activities
* Make the Supplier Association our vehicle to ensure teamwork

Suppliers

Trico will focus business with suppliers committed to continuous improvement and proactive relationship who share our goal of World Class status.

Our suppliers will be encouraged through our Supplier Association mechanism to:

* Work with us in an open cooperative way involving all functions
* Improve continuously supply logistics to deliver frequently to the point of use:
  —guaranteed quality
  —guaranteed quantity
  —on time, every time
* Provide active involvement in our design processes to:
  —optimize materials, processes and tooling
  —reduce costs, delays and lead times

* Actively participate in target costing, value analysis and cost reduction programs
* Contribute to effective and timely communications across all functions
* Develop a culture of continual improvement and elimination of waste from all processes
* Introduce EDI and CAD links where appropriate
* Be capable of growth and diversification to support future business needs
* Strive for quality and excellence in all activities

(80 percent) of Trico's purchases. They ranged from plastic and rubber raw material and parts makers to metal processors and packaging suppliers. During the one-day conference Trico's strategies were explained by the top management team, the concept of the supplier association was explained, and a proposed working framework was presented by Taylor based on the strategy document.

After lunch the suppliers were split into groups and asked to give their views. There was, of course, a good degree of weariness and some concern about what the work would achieve. However, with Morris's guidance, Taylor was able to persuade all the suppliers to buy in to the process and to agree to take part in the two types of benchmarking. The first type, called continuous improvement benchmarking, measured nine key attributes concerned with quality, productivity, and delivery performance. This was designed to produce hard data that could be used for targeting future performances. When this benchmarking was applied to the companies (including Trico), however, a problem soon arose. Namely, most of the companies were not even recording some aspects of their day-to-day performance and had trouble even understanding one or two of the questions. As a result, any attempt to agree on hard targets would be next to impossible, so that was not done at this stage.

❖ Most of the companies were not even recording some aspects of their day-to-day performance and had trouble even understanding one or two of the questions.

The second type of benchmarking, called supplier capability benchmarking, was also used. This involved staff from Trico facilitating round-table management discussions at each supplier location to diagnose the company's internal processes. This was very time-consuming for Trico and took longer than expected. The method was used to find out whether each company (again, including Trico) had the processes in place to achieve world-class performance. Unfortunately, this turned out not to be the case. A matrix was drawn up showing in which areas the individual companies were deficient. To maintain anonymity, the different companies involved were identified by specific letters.

These findings were brought back to the suppliers at the inaugural seminar, held in June 1995. The general reaction was a restless, "Well, what do we do next?" Taylor and Morris already had a plan in place but did not want to impose a scheme on the suppliers that they had not originated. Trico had suffered from its customers' doing this over the years, and Taylor and Morris did not want to make that mistake. The result of the discussion at the seminar was inconclusive as a result, and the suppliers went away unsure about what would happen. This was a make-or-break time for the association.

Shortly afterward, Taylor brought the suppliers together again after talking to most of them on a one-on-one basis and getting their viewpoints. At this next meeting the House of Lean Production was introduced as an operating framework to implement the various improvements identified in the development matrix. This system, represented schematically as the facade of a columned building (see Figure 13.2), was suggested by Morris as a compilation of his views about the way world-class performance had been created in companies like Toyota.

After further discussion, the suppliers accepted the House of Lean Production as a viable framework. To Taylor's relief, a plan was drawn up to implement the needed changes, and he announced that he was not going to ask the group to undertake any activities that Trico was not willing to undertake. As a first step, a very basic "5S" housekeeping program was suggested. This meant gaining control over the simplest things, such as cleaning machines or tidying up so

13.2. The House of Lean Production.

The program consists of six stages, schematized as follows:

Stage 6:

Stage 5:
Stage 4:

Stage 3:

Stage 2:
Stage 1:

Stage 1:   "5S" – A five-step process designed to put day-to-day order in a company:
a. clearing up
b. sorting out
c. organizing
d. cleaning
e. disciplining

Stage 2:   Structured problem-solving techniques that allow a company to diagnose a problem and to identify and prioritize solutions

Stage 3:   Four pillars of expertise are taught:
a. delivery (*kanban* methods)
b. waste control
c. maintenance
d. right first-time and visual management

Step 4:   Planning and scheduling capabilities

Step 5:   Continuous improvement as a way of doing business

Step 6:   Process management as a strategy

that the causes of disorder could at least become visible. "Once this firm bedrock is in place" Taylor suggested, "we can go on to develop a *kanban*-based delivery system." Unfortunately, the mere mention of *kanban* set a deadly pall over the suppliers. "You could see the blinders go up," Morris said later, "and the morale and self-belief of the firms disappear. They were clearly not ready to embark on a *kanban* program without first developing more trust."

❖ A very basic "5S" housekeeping program was suggested. This meant gaining control over the simplest things, such as cleaning machines or tidying up so that the causes of disorder could at least become visible.

The situation improved when one of the suppliers suggested that they just concentrate on 5S housekeeping at this stage and worry about *kanbans* later. By the end of the meeting a 5S implementation plan was developed. The plan employed the Deming Plan Do Check Act (PDCA) improvement cycle. When put into practice this cycle took around six months to complete. It consisted of an initial seminar for senior managers held at Trico in August 1995 to help each company understand the basics of 5S and commit to action. This was followed by a more detailed training workshop in October 1995 for operations staff, held at supplier's company. Following this, each company was asked to pilot a 5S project. All except one supplier did this. Trico took the lead with immediate positive results.

A sense of initiative permeates the company. The reason is that Jim Taylor leads not only the supplier association activities but also the internal 5S activities throughout the company. To date thirty-three 5S groups have been started, involving around a third of the 500-plus workforce. The first of these to be started was in the purchasing office. Taylor does not ask suppliers to do things before he and his team have tried them.

The result is that the purchasing department, part of a large open-plan office, is extremely well organized. When asked if he has any information on the Quest group, Taylor pulls out two folders and within seconds can produce the exact piece of paper required. This was not the case before becoming involved in 5S. Taylor mentions in passing that just after the 5S work started there was "much peering over walls, and people came from right across the site to look at my desk. It was so clear that they thought I must have left!" The same attitude and attention to detail is now apparent wherever you go inside the company. In a few short months the 5S work had transformed the organization and the culture of the workforce. This is now a company that is capable of becoming a world leader, and it has a group of suppliers to help it on the journey.

❖ In a few short months the 5S work had transformed the organization and the culture of the workforce. This is now a company that is capable of becoming a world leader, and it has a group of suppliers to help it on the journey.

Trico's experiences in its 5S work as well as those of the operational staffs from the other companies was shared at a workshop in January 1996. This progress was brought back to the senior managers at a further meeting in February 1996. At this seminar the atmosphere was quite different from that of earlier meetings. With the exception of the one company that had not really made progress, everyone could see the benefits of working together. One benefit was that suppliers no longer resisted Jim Taylor's renewed suggestion that they implement a *kanban* delivery system. They knew, this time, that Trico would take the lead. As a result, a *kanban* awareness, learning, and implementation program was launched.

IMPRESSIONS TO DATE

Taylor sits back in his chair and appears to echo the message given from Rover some months before as he suggests that the supplier association has been "extremely beneficial (with) results now showing—the best vehicle we have seen for communicating to a group of suppliers." Asked for an example but rather humble about his own achievements, he tells us about a plastic supplier: "The quality of product improved as soon as they started their 5S activity in the warehouse. It resulted in a major time saving for the team leader who could then address various quality issues for product being shipped to us. As a result quality has improved almost overnight." Although not eager to give exact details, a tour around the factory reveals shelves cleared of idle inventory. In another location storage racks have been removed completely. A glance at one of numerous charts on the purchasing office walls shows the cumulative yearly price changes for suppliers being a negative figure. Things seem to be under control and getting better.

In addition, word of mouth spread news of the early success, and the American sister company decided to launch its own group. Already, a twenty-five-member-strong supplier association has been formed. In addition, one of Trico's Quest members, fueled by the enthusiasm and success grown out of working with Trico, is starting its own group.

 "I realized that by and large we needed a vehicle to create improvement and that the days of rattling cages and threatening suppliers was ended."

Summing up his impression of the work, David Jones commented, "I didn't come on board that quickly at first because I was not totally convinced, (but I realized that) by and large we needed a vehicle to create improvement and that the days of rattling cages and threatening suppliers was ended. What's more," he added, "we enjoy it and we encourage the suppliers to constructively criticize us as much as we do them, and they do!" He continued by stressing the internal improvements and relationships that have been built as a result of the work: "We're trying to change the philosophy here. With the enthusiasm generated from the 5S program here, the main problem now is fighting people off who want to take part!"

PLANNING FOR THE FUTURE

The implementation of a *kanban* system with suppliers is the next major activity for the Trico Quest Supplier Association. After this it says it might rebenchmark and be in a position to set far more specific and measurable targets. It also has to consider what to do with the rest of its suppliers, although a less comprehensive supplier development program is already in place.

In 1992, Trico lay at the threshold of a new cycle of productivity gains. Achieving it depended on having a modern factory with world-class production facilities and methods, a new organizational culture, and a better supplier base. The new Pontypool facility provided the physical structure. However, the newly constituted supplier association set in place the foundations for a new way of doing business by building a shared-learning system with its suppliers. Rather unexpectedly, it helped provide a framework for a dynamic and innovation-minded business behavior at Trico.

PART V

Lifting
the
Bar

Chapter 14

BAMBOO TO COMPOSITES

As the ecological, economic and political problems of mankind have become global, complex, and non-linear, the traditional concept of individual responsibility is questionable. We need new models of collective behavior depending on the different degrees of our individual faculties and insights.

Klaus Mainzer, *Thinking in Complexity,* 2d ed.
(New York: Springer-Verlag, 1996), p. 315

In Chapter 3, the analogy was made between the world of sports and the way in which a three-tier teaming system functions. We return to that analogy to reinforce a central theme of this book. Forty years ago, the pole-vaulter used a bamboo pole to reach world records measured at fourteen to fifteen feet. The athlete in those times was most likely to be a devoted amateur working with limited resources and serving as his own trainer, coach, and expert resource. Less than thirty years later, the competitive environment was unrecognizable. Winning heights had reached in excess of twenty feet, and the preferred material for poles was an exotic composite of carbon fibers. For pole-vaulters, victory would be settled in fractions of inches, while in other sports it would be measured in hundredths of seconds or in thousandths of points. And while the individual vaulter still remained the focus of attention as he floated over the delicately balanced horizontal bar, training had become a lengthy, costly process involving a widening variety of highly specialized skills and tools. During that period, too, sports were transformed into a growth-minded multi-billion-dollar industry with global markets for soccer championships and Olympic games.

Performance metrics are a centerpiece to the analogy. The victory-minded athlete is driven by a need to win medals, by precise and measurable gaps that must be narrowed to achieve a winning performance, and by day-to-day measures of improvements and training. In a corporate setting, at each of the three organizational levels described in the three-tier system, metrics play as vital a role as they do for the athlete. They provide the reference points against which to calibrate actions and progress. The innovation shared in this book is in the building of process-focused performance gaps as a bridge between business objectives and day-to-day actions.

Business has moved forward from "bamboo" to "composites" in a knowledge-intensive, highly competitive, and global business world. It is one in which performance gaps differentiating winners from losers evolved in a few decades, from parts per thousand to parts per billion, and now to parts per trillion. Sustaining such geometric rates of improvement has put a premium on the knowledge intensity built into solutions. But with the high cost of knowledge-driven progress comes levels of high investments, making risk of failure itself a high-stakes game for investors, managers, and employees.

As explained in the opening chapters, business success in a far more complex economy calls for treating problems and opportunities systemically—hence, the importance of a new set of holistic management skills and the paradoxical recognition that control over increasing complexity comes through ever simpler solutions. It is in this context that leading companies are abandoning their bamboo organizational antecedents that once served them well to vault fourteen-foot heights. This explains a change from structure-bound strategies in which functions were the main players to ones that are process driven and in which teams focus their efforts on meeting customer needs. Hence the new managerial composite aimed at taming ever more complex value-adding chains. This was seen in companies like Tesco that evolved in a short period from a mom-and-pop retail distribution chain into a finely tuned logistical system capable of managing information and deliveries in real time across a larger and more demanding network of stores and customers. The composite is in the intermeshing of competencies into smoothly operating teams that not only fully comprehend the whole process but are given complete responsibility over it. The whole in such cases is much stronger than any individual part, thereby yielding greater performance and productivity. Creating transparency in any one part of an organization is a key to building a whole system that can be seen through any one of its parts.

❖ The composite is in the intermeshing of competencies into smoothly operating teams that not only fully comprehend the whole process but are given complete responsibility over it. The whole in such cases is much stronger than any individual part, thereby yielding greater performance and productivity.

Behind this new teaming composite is the three-tier system of management that fuels a highly performing system aligned around a vital few core processes. Critical to its success, too, is an appreciation of a very different kind of organizational behavior. We describe it as nonlinear in that interactions between members of such teams—and between teams themselves—are open and accessible as opposed to task-driven and controlled. The managerial skill is to keep it focused and directed. This was illustrated in Chapter 4 by the CEO of Otikon, who talked about his responsibility to keep his company alive by keeping it "dis-organized." Nonlinear behavioral is essential to creative and adaptive organizations. The goal is to tap the creative potential that flows out of such nonlinearity and seeming chaos and from it deliver increased value to the buyer of a product or service.

There is in this nonlinearity a renewed appreciation of the critical role information plays as a competitive resource. As electronic commerce networks, distributed databases, and desktop computers become ubiquitous, the challenge is in knowing how to extract value from an almost infinitely deep information pool. More effective decision management has emerged, as a result, as a critical facet of effective process management. Learning to better support teams with real-time information that enhances both their judgment and decision-making ability is at the frontier of management. The startling pace at which this is evolving was capsulized by Andy Grove, Intel's CEO, when quoted in Chapter 3 as measuring compressed Silicon Valley time in "web-weeks."

This new awareness of process mastery as a defining quality of a competitive strategy is a perceptual breakthrough along an evolutionary path. It recognizes, in part, that it is not so much *what* is produced that distinguishes winners from losers but *how* it is produced. Some of the early steps were first taken by the gurus of the quality movement, such as W. Edwards Deming, Dr. A. V. Feigenbaum, and Joseph Juran, who understood the power of mastery over process. Deming once said that America's competitive recovery required optimization of the whole system. Quality, in his view, meant maximal usefulness to the market, a concept keenly admonished by another guru, Peter Drucker, who argued in the mid-1950s that the purpose of a business is "to create customers." Out of this concept he coined the phrase "the marketing concept" to mean the delivery of the whole business in the service of the customer. This, he understood at the time—and Japanese companies learned from him— could only be achieved by abandoning a functional structure to one that managed whole processes. Toyota and Komatsu put such learnings into practice in the early 1960s through a structure of cross-functional processes that would not be appreciated as a management breakthrough in the United States until some twenty-five years later. The 1990s have been a period of rapid maturation toward a process-focused strategy by Western organizations, an evolution fueled by the concurrent engineering movement and later by a rapid embracing of process reengineering as a stepping-stone toward leaner and more adaptive business performance.

But if the 1990s have taught the corporate world anything, it is the hard lesson that cost reduction efforts—headlined by a wave of downsizing programs at companies like AT&T, GM, Procter &

Gamble, and almost every other large company—is the easy part of the equation, often achieved at hidden, longer-term systemic costs. The nonlinear vitality of a company, from which new ideas germinate, is often stripped out of the company by misapplied business process reengineering programs. With it goes the creativity upon which new growth is founded. Hence, the accelerating interest in process management as a systemic approach to managing growth in an ever more complex global economy.

The story of this evolution was shared through the experiences of several companies and industries spanning continents. That some of these illustrative cases are drawn from Wales, a region that was until recently noted mostly for its spirited rugby songs and its dying coal-mining culture, is testimony to the title of this chapter. Wales, small as it is, is a laboratory of industrial change induced by global economic forces. The particulars expressed by visionary managers such as Alan Kirkham, the Managing Director of Mitel, speak to a far larger community of companies worldwide. The future, as he sees it, is shaping itself around those that not only see the power of knowledge as a competitive resource but who are able to tap it through composite behaviors and thus exhibit process excellence.

A CHECKLIST FOR SUPPLIER ASSOCIATION SUCCESS

Note. This section is designed as a checklist for those interested in creating their own supplier association. Each of the ten stages of this approach are discussed in turn. The ten stages were drawn from Peter Hines, "A New Route to the Creation of World Class Suppliers," in *Creating World Class Suppliers: Unlocking Mutual Advantage* (London: Pitman Publishing, 1994).

1. Benchmark Your Present Competitive Position

The first stage is to understand the starting point from which your company decided to integrate further with its existing supplier base. This is best achieved by benchmarking yourselves against the ideals of your customers. In this way the company will not only be able to focus its internal efforts but those of their suppliers as well. Such companywide benchmarking should be accompanied by a similar benchmarking of the company's existing relationship with its suppliers. In this way the organization can judge where its supply process fits by the world's best standards and which policies it may usefully pursue.

2. Select Appropriate Coordination and Development Tools

As a result of the benchmarking of the organization and its supply arrangements, the company will gain a feel for where it strategically sits. It can then select the appropriate strategies and operational tools to integrate with its suppliers.

A supplier association is appropriate for those organizations that have already made significant progress in their supplier integration activities. Examples of such progress include: the adoption of yearly supplier conferences, the use of supplier audits and the implementation of a supplier development program. Companies that are not already undertaking such work will either not be ready or will be unaware of the benefits of the more sophisticated approach described here.

3. Gain Internal Acceptance and Create Cross-Functional Team

Once a decision has been made to organize a supplier association, companywide support is essential. It is also important to form an implementation team that is cross-functional in nature so that the key processes that run across functional and company boundaries can be adequately addressed. "Without an articulated interdepartmental coordination mechanism," Japanese academic Toshihiro Nishiguchi points out, "incumbent departments are prone to be myopically concerned with their own narrowly focused transactions."[1] To avoid this problem, you can use the following five-step approach.

a. Establish the management environment.

To gain consistency of purpose over an extended period of time it is necessary to establish the right managerial environment for the successful implementation process. The right environment requires top management support to ensure that the work fits within the overall strategic direction of the company. Such commitment will help motivate other company members and help to avoid suboptimal function through political infighting.

b. Develop cross-functional team.

It is important that the supplier association is a cross-functional activity because it involves the coordination and development of the whole range of functions of the suppliers. In addition, a cross-functional approach will help the supplier association to be viewed as a key part of a company's strategy rather than simply a purchasing activity. The cross-functional team, possibly headed by a purchaser, is likely to contain representatives from marketing, quality, design, manufacturing, and accounting, although other functions may also be represented, as may one or more key suppliers or customers.

c. Gain an understanding of the company's requirements and those of its customers.

It is important that purchasing, if it is to lead this work, develop a proper understanding of what the company wishes to do and how its customers' requirements need to be fulfilled. This understanding is essential if this knowledge is to be passed on to the suppliers. A simplified version of the VALSAT approach, explained in Chapter 12, may be useful. This would involve working with internal and external customers to ensure that customer requirements can be captured and activities put in place to satisfy these needs.

d. Train the cross-functional team.

A cross-functional team training program is necessary so that all of the members understand: the role of the supplier association, how the supplier association may be implemented, their individual roles in the work, and the benefits that are likely to be yielded to their own company and those of the participating suppliers.

e. Create implementation plans.

The team should work on its implementation plan. The most appropriate mechanism for this planning process is the cross-organization process map.[3] This map should be used to reflect the individual customer requirements and solutions discussed above. The map produced will be unique to the individual company but will depict the cross-functional team, the key implementation stages, the individual tasks and who is to carry them out, as well as the key review points and control standards. This tool will help aid the rigorous implementation process and therefore increase the benefits from the resultant supplier association.

4. Select Appropriate Suppliers

To start a supplier association it is necessary to select the inaugural membership from among the customer company's total supplier base. In general, at least at the early stages, membership should be limited to a small group of not more than fifteen companies so that the activities and membership can be kept both focused and manageable. This selection may be a simple process if membership is offered to existing preferred suppliers. However, if no such system exists, a number of criteria may be taken into account in making this choice. Some of these are:

- The proximity of the supplier
- The yearly cash spent with each supplier
- The degree of closeness of the existing relationship
- The degree to which the supplier provides unique products
- The degree to which the supplier provides key parts or parts that have a large design input
- The degree to which the supplier is willing to invest in people, tools, machinery, and factory space dedicated to its customer requirements.
- The general enthusiasm of the supplier for the business relationship and the supplier association in particular
- The degree of progressiveness of the supplier's management and the managers' ability to innovate and share their experiences

This list is not exhaustive but will provide a useful guide in deciding which companies should be invited into the supplier association. After this selection process has occurred individual suppliers should be invited to take part in the association. This is best achieved through an introductory seminar to which all the selected suppliers are invited to attend. The meeting can be used to discuss the details of the supplier association and how it can be employed by the customer to all of the members' mutual benefit.

5. Benchmark Supplier Position

The first activity within the association should be a benchmarking of the individual members to ascertain their present strategies, skills, and application of leading-edge tools and techniques. This benchmark should be carried out with all the member companies, including the customers. Such an effort will help indicate how good each company is at the key deliverables that the customer is interested in, such as order fulfillment, quality, and productivity. This could be compared with the requirements of the customer company as well as the customer's own customer, as this will already be known from the VALSAT exercise.

The result of this benchmark plotting is that both buyer and supplier can see what gaps exist and can therefore make plans to make improvements within the association's activities or individually. If many of the suppliers have the same problems, a joint program can be put into place.

6. Jointly Target Improvements

At this stage it would be too easy to take the gap between present performance and that required by the customer and give the supplier a fixed time to close the gap. However, this would be dangerous for a number of reasons. First, such an approach takes no account of where the customer wants the supplier to be in, for instance, twelve months' time. More important, no attention is paid to whether such an undertaking is realistic and reasonable to ask of a supplier. It also takes no account of the type of assistance that the supplier may require nor the amount of effort the customer or other suppliers are prepared to give. Last, such a blanket approach may not encourage a supplier that is already very good in one deliverable to become world class in this area.

As a result a more pragmatic approach should be used, such as the half-life predictive metric tool developed by Art Schneiderman (explained in Chapter 5).[4] This will help avoid underachievement because of undertargeting. It will also discourage overambitious targets that are unattainable and will only result in failure and possible dissension between buyer and supplier. Allow the targets to be jointly focused using half-life time frames; then strict, predictable, and achievable targets may be set and reached.

7. Focus Coordination and Development Efforts

It is essential to fine-tune the focus and direction of the group at this stage. The broad focus has already been achieved through the VALSAT work coupled with the benchmarking and targeting exercises. However, by a detailed mapping of the possible programs necessary to achieve these goals, a more rounded program can be produced.

In addition to development and training in the relevant operational tools and techniques, it is also important that the group is used for supplier coordination. The best method of coordinating a supplier network is to share long-term strategies between the individual members so that a clear long-term synergistic relationship can be built to the advantage of all concerned. This area of strategy sharing should be more than just the customer sharing its own strategies, but should also involve a forum for a similar flow from the suppliers to the customers and even between suppliers if various commonalities and synergies become apparent.

8. Undertake Group Activities

The focusing of the coordination and development efforts is the last stage in setting up the supplier association. It forms the "doing" stage. The format of the activities as well as the subject matter covered by the association will vary from group to group. However, the following types of activities are common in the most successful group in the United Kingdom:

- Yearly conferences primarily used by the customer to share its future strategic direction as well as more detailed operational plans. The type of information shared at such a meeting is likely to include: future product and marketing strategies, development of new processes or factory space, financial results, new business opportunities under discussion, and concerns in the supplier area.
- At a lower level, a seminar series involving from four to six events a year. This group should include senior staff from the suppliers and be used to share information with suppliers that is of a strategic nature. It should also play a role in continually refocusing activities within the group. The last role is, in a more operational sense, that of sharing information and contents of the various tools and techniques to be used in the supplier association. Such sharing should not only involve explanation but also interactive group discussion so that the full implications of implementation can be explored.
- At the third operational level, required meetings of line staff from member companies in order to understand in detail the new tools, techniques, and strategies to be pursued by association members. Because not every tool, technique, or skill discussed at the seminars by senior management will be applicable to member companies, the attendance of these specific workshops is likely to involve only a subset of the whole group. However, these companies can play a vital role in helping the other companies by regularly reporting progress

at future seminar events. This may encourage additional informal networking between member companies.

- A regular newsletter that can be used to keep members, as well as nonmembers, aware of developments by the customer and the key suppliers.
- A series of visits to exemplar companies to help other suppliers emulate the best practice exhibited.
- Social events to help improve the informal ties between members as well as generally build trust and a common sense of purpose.

9. Measure Improvements

The ninth stage in the creation of a supplier association is the check stage, that of the measurement of individual and collective progress. This measurement should be done on a regular basis, perhaps twice yearly. It should involve a detailed one-to-one discussion between customer and supplier as to how far the latter has gone in meeting its jointly agreed target. This may also involve the customer's being made aware of the problems it is causing the supplier. If progress has not been as rapid as required, this regular measurement can mean that remedial plans can be put in place either on an individual basis or a joint basis.

In addition to the measurement of these targets, a review should be conducted regularly to gauge the benefits being achieved through the supplier association. A regular review of activities by customers and suppliers alike will help to improve the focus and benefits achieved through group activities. It will therefore help not only to improve the coordination and development of suppliers but also the process of improvement itself.

10. Refocus Size of Group and Target Areas

As a result of the measurement carried out in the last stage, the group can refocus. This is the action stage. It can involve any area of group activities that would lead to increased competitive advantage. Thus a new area for development may be targeted, new criteria for measurement created, or the size of the group increased to accommodate new suppliers. This refocusing should be carried out on a regular basis, either at every seminar meeting or perhaps every six months. Such checkpoints would also include taking stock of the changing requirements of the customer company or of the marketplace.

Once such refocusing has occurred, the cycle of Plan Do Check Act should be repeated. There should be a loop back to stage 5 with a reiteration of the benchmarking, targeting, focusing of activities, activity completion, measurement, and group checking. The cycle would then be repeated with an improvement of the process achieved with each reiteration.

NOTES

1. Toshihiro Nishiguchi, "Reforming Automative Purchasing Organization in North America: Lessons for Europe?" International Motor Vehicle Program Conference, Como, Italy, 15–18 May, 1988.
2. The value stream analysis tool (VALSAT) is described in more detail in Peter Hines, Nick Rich, and Malaika Hittmeyer, "Competing Against Ignorance: Advantage Through Knowledge," *International Journal of Physical Distribution and Logistics Management,* vol. 17, no. 1, 1997.
3. One kind of mapping method—four fields maps—appropriate to cross-functional teaming is described by Dan Dimancescu in *The Seamless Enterprise: Making Cross-Functional Management Work* (New York: Wiley, 1994).
4. For a detailed description see Brian Maskell, *Performance Measurement for World Class Manufacturing: A Model for American Companies* (Portland, Oreg.: Productivity Press, 1991).

INDEX